The
MODERN
COOK'S
Cookbook

The
MODERN
COOK'S
Cookbook

Kathy Man

Photographs by Nick Carman

Produced for The Tupperware Company by Good Books (GB Publications Limited) Lagard Farm, Whitley, Wilts SN12 8RL

Copyright © The Tupperware Company 1991

ISBN 0 946555 20 6 (softcover)
     0 946555 21 4 (hardcover)

Microwave recipes created by Rosemary Moon
Photography on pages 6, 8, 10 by Simon Smith

Project planner: Claire Osborne
Editor: Helen Slater
Associate editors: Elvira Romans, Ros Tarrant
Design and typesetting: Baseline Creative, Bath
Cover design: Lloyd Northover, London
Art director: Charlie Goodley
Stylist: Maria Jacques
Illustrations: Tom Cross

Colour separation by Fotographics Ltd, London and Hong Kong
Made and printed in Great Britain by Butler & Tanner Ltd, Frome

The Tupperware Company
Tupperware House
130 College Road
Harrow
Middlesex HAl lBQ

CONTENTS

TUPPERWARE FOR THE MODERN COOK

The Modern Cook's Cookbook is a celebration of good tastes, delicate flavours, fresh ingredients and imaginative cooking. It is also a celebration of the modern cook's ability to produce delicious food simply and relatively quickly, when necessary. Few women wish, or are able, to spend a day slaving over a hot stove. An uncomplicated, but healthy and delicious meal, swiftly conjured up in the hour after getting in from work, is more likely to be the norm.

We are fortunate these days in having an ever-increasing supply of exotic, and tempting, fresh ingredients from all over the world. Travel abroad, and increased interest in the cuisines of other countries, means that we are more adventurous in our cooking as well as our eating. We are no longer bound by any one style of food. The only criteria are those of taste and budget.

Influencing both of these is the modern awareness of healthy eating. There is a new emphasis on lighter meals, more salads, vegetables of all kinds, and less emphasis on red meats and cholesterol-rich foods. This has created a myriad of taste sensations. We use herbs and garlic and spices more. We look to the quality of the ingredients and aim to bring out the natural flavours, rather than cover everything in heavy sauces. This is surprisingly economical and healthy as any vegetable (other than a truffle) costs far less than most meats.

Quality and freshness is something that Tupperware has been identified with for over 30 years. People in 42 countries worldwide associate the company with excellence, and a superb product range. Generations have grown up with Tupperware, and hundreds of thousands of women have found the products' space-saving, time-saving, and labour-saving qualities invaluable when they have to balance the demands of career and work with home and family.

Tupperware are very aware of the needs and demands of changing lifestyles. We need more organised kitchens, so we can operate more efficiently with the time and space that we have. We need to use our freezers and microwaves more effectively, and finally, we want to be able to present our food attractively and effortlessly.

For every one of these problems, Tupperware has a solution.

Organising your kitchen couldn't be easier – the Tupperware storage range is legendary. It comes in a wide selection of shapes and sizes that are all modular, so they build and stack to fit any cupboard space exactly; 'windows' allow you to see contents at a glance, while the unique airtight seal (invented by Earl Tupper over 45 years ago) keeps food really fresh.

As for fridge and freezer, Tupperware high quality products are not only specially designed, but made from a particularly flexible material guaranteed for life not to become brittle or crack in extremes of temperature. There is also a superb new microwave range, as well as a wide variety of excellent preparation and serving products, all designed to minimise your work and maximise the most important thing of all – your pleasure in cooking.

The recipes that follow have taken account of the very varied lifestyles that we lead today. There are recipes for simple healthy family meals, as well as lighter dishes suitable for the slimmer. There are recipes for packed lunches and picnics, barbecues, children's parties and delicious desserts. The savouries and snacks would all make original and tempting accompaniments for drinks parties, while the recipes in the soups and starters and main course sections all provide delightful and enticing glimpses of Mediterranean, Eastern and Oriental influences.

It is a book guaranteed to inspire and delight you and, hopefully, tempt you to try ingredients and dishes that you have not tasted before. Each recipe is clearly and simply explained, as well as fully illustrated, so that even a novice cook would be able to use the book with confidence.

If variety is indeed the spice of life, *The Modern Cook's Cookbook* should provide you with an abundance of new flavours to experiment with, and enjoy, in the months and years to come.

Bon appétit!

NOTES

✎ Quantities are given in both metric and Imperial measures. In converting from Imperial to metric, we have rounded the figure up or down to give a practical working quantity. Always follow only one set of measures as they are not interchangeable. (See conversion tables and oven temperatures below.)

✎ All the microwave recipes have been tested on a 700W microwave cooker. If your oven has a lower wattage, refer to the chart below. All times given are approximate – check your food regularly during cooking.

✎ The calorie count in each recipe, which is based on the metric measurement, serves as a guide only. If you are on a strict dietary regime you should make your own precise calculations.

✎ The number of servings for each recipe is based on average appetites. Adjustments should be made for light or hearty eaters.

✎ All eggs are size 3 unless otherwise stated.

✎ Spoon measures are level unless otherwise stated.

✎ Cooking margarine can be substituted for butter in all recipes.

✎ There are a number of slightly more challenging recipes in the book which are particularly suitable for those special occasions when, as a cook, you want to pull out all the stops. These are indicated by a chef's hat symbol.

CONVERSION TABLES

WEIGHT CONVERSIONS

Imperial	Metric
$^1/_2$oz	15g
1oz	25g
3oz	75g
4oz	100g
5oz	150g
6oz	175g
7oz	200g
8oz	225g
9oz	250g
10oz	275g
11oz	300g
12oz	350g
13oz	375g
14oz	400g
15oz	425g
16oz (1lb)	450g

LIQUID CONVERSIONS

Imperial	Metric
1fl oz	25ml
2fl oz	50ml
3fl oz	75ml
4fl oz	100ml
5fl oz/$^1/_4$ pint	150ml
10fl oz/$^1/_2$ pint	300ml
15fl oz/$^3/_4$ pint	450ml
20fl oz/1 pint	600ml

MICROWAVE
Use this chart to adjust cooking times for lower wattage ovens.

650/700 Watt	600 Watt	500 Watt
30 sec	35 sec	40 sec
1 min	1 min 10	1 min 20
2 min	2 min 30	3 min
3 min	3 min 30	4 min
4 min	4 min 30	5 min
5 min	6 min	6 min 30
10 min	11 min 30	13 min
15 min	17 min	20 min
20 min	23 min	26 min
30 min	35 min	39 min

OVEN TEMPERATURES

C	F	Gas Mark
110	225	$^1/_4$
130	250	$^1/_2$
140	275	1
150	300	2
175	325	3
180	350	4
190	375	5
200	400	6
220	425	7
230	450	8
240	475	9

1
Soups and Starters

In 1945 American chemist Earl Tupper invented a unique airtight seal for plastic containers. This was the start of Tupperware, which was to change the face of kitchenware, first in the USA and then throughout the rest of the world. Equally revolutionary was the decision to sell the products via Tupperware parties in the home, where they could be properly demonstrated, rather than through retail outlets in the conventional way.

Although prepared dips should be stored in the fridge, they will taste a lot better if you let them come to room temperature before serving.

AVOCADO AND LEMON SOUP

Preparation time : 15 minutes
Plus chilling time : 2 hours
Calories per serving : 90

•

2 small lemons
1 large ripe avocado
600ml (1 pint) cold vegetable stock (page 126)
150ml (1/4 pint) Greek yogurt
salt and freshly ground black pepper
2tbsp Greek yogurt for garnish

1. Use the fine grater in the Cook's Maid to remove the zest from the lemons. Reserve for garnishing. Convert the Cook's Maid into a juicer and squeeze out the juice.
2. Halve the avocado, remove the stone, scoop out the flesh and chop it roughly.
3. Blend the avocado flesh, lemon juice and half the stock in a liquidiser or food processor for 1 minute. Add the remainder of the stock, yogurt and seasoning, and blend for a further 30 seconds.
4. Transfer to a 1.5 litre Bowl, seal and chill for 2 hours before serving.
5. Serve with a swirl of yogurt and sprinkle with grated lemon zest to enhance the delicate flavour of the soup.

Serves 4

This soup is also delicious served warm, but be careful not to boil it as this brings out the bitterness in the avocado. To give it a truly Greek flavour, eat with hot garlic pitta bread.

SMOKED SALMON AND PISTACHIO TIMBALES

Preparation time : 25 minutes
Chilling time : 1 hour
Calories per serving : 195

•

350g (12oz) smoked salmon, thinly sliced
100g (4oz) cream cheese
100g (4oz) fromage frais
25g (1oz) shelled pistachio nuts
1tbsp finely chopped fresh dill (or 1tsp dried)
salt and freshly ground black pepper
fresh dill and lemon slices for garnish

1. Cut 16 strips of smoked salmon each approximately 2.5cm x 20cm (1in x 8in) and use to line four Colourfun Snack Cups. The salmon will hang over the sides.
2. Blend the cream cheese and fromage frais in a liquidiser or food processor for 1 minute. Add the remainder of the salmon, pistachio nuts, dill and seasoning and blend for a further 30 seconds.
3. Spoon into the prepared Colourfun Snack Cups and fold the overlapping salmon over the cheese mixture. Seal and chill for 1 hour.
4. Turn out on to individual serving plates and garnish with dill and thinly cut lemon slices.

Serves 4

SPINACH BEIGNETS WITH CHILLI DIP

Preparation time : 15 minutes
Cooking time : 20 minutes
Calories per serving : 375-562

•

150ml (1/4 pint) cold water
50g (2oz) butter
1/2 tsp salt
60g (2 1/2 oz) plain flour
2 eggs, lightly shaken in the Quick Shake
225g (8oz) cooked spinach (frozen or fresh),
squeezed dry and chopped
oil for deep frying
150ml (1/4 pint) mayonnaise
2tbsp tomato ketchup
large pinch chilli powder (or to taste)

1. Place the water, butter and salt in a saucepan and bring to the boil. Remove pan from heat and immediately add all the flour, stirring it into the mixture vigorously.
2. Beat the mixture until it forms a ball of smooth paste, then add the egg a little at a time. Beat thoroughly in between each addition. Add the spinach and continue to beat thoroughly.
3. Heat the oil until a cube of bread will sizzle in it. Drop teaspoonfuls of the spinach mixture into the fat and fry until brown and crisp. Drain using the Colander Server inside a 3 litre Bowl. Repeat until all the mixture is used up.

TOP *Spinach Beignets with Chilli Dip* CENTRE *Avocado & Lemon Soup* BOTTOM *Smoked Salmon & Pistachio Timbales*

TOP *Smoked Haddock Mousse Pancakes* CENTRE *Oriental Chicken & Mushroom Soup* BOTTOM *Quails' Eggs with Avocado Sauce*

14

4. To serve, mix the mayonnaise with the tomato ketchup and chilli powder and pour into the centre of the Party Server. Arrange the beignets around it.

Makes approximately 24
Serves 4-6

Prepared beignets may be frozen in a Freeze n Stor for several months. Simply reheat from frozen in a hot oven.

ORIENTAL CHICKEN AND MUSHROOM SOUP

Preparation time : 5 minutes
Cooking time : 35 minutes
Calories per serving : 45

•

100g (4oz) chicken breast fillet
900ml (1 ¹/₂ pints) chicken stock (page 126)
100g (4oz) shiitake mushrooms, thinly sliced
salt and ground white pepper
1tsp sesame oil
1tbsp chopped spring onions

1. Place the chicken and stock in a saucepan, bring to the boil, then cover and simmer for 20 minutes.
2. Remove the chicken, slice thinly and divide between 4 Oriental Bowls. Line a Double Colander with a piece of clean muslin and strain the cooking liquid into a clean saucepan.
3. Add the mushrooms and bring to the boil. Cover and simmer for 10 minutes.
4. Adjust seasoning, add the sesame oil and, using a Kitchen Duo Ladle, spoon the soup over the chicken. Sprinkle with chopped spring onions before serving.

Serves 4

Reconstituted dried Chinese mushrooms or any other type of wild or cultivated mushrooms will work equally well, but the flavour of the soup will vary accordingly.

Eat with Chicken and Sesame Toasts (see page 85).

QUAILS' EGGS WITH AVOCADO SAUCE

Preparation time : 20 minutes
Calories per serving : 84

•

100g (4oz) white cabbage
12 quails' eggs, hard-boiled
¹/₂ small ripe avocado
2tbsp freshly squeezed lime juice
4tbsp plain yogurt
1tsp chopped fresh chervil (or ¹/₄ tsp dried)
salt and freshly ground black pepper

1. Slice the cabbage finely and divide between 4 individual plates. Arrange to form 'nests'.
2. Shell the quails' eggs, cut each in half lengthwise and place 6 halves inside each cabbage nest.
3. Scoop out the flesh from the avocado. Then chop the avocado into chunks and blend in a liquidiser or food processor together with the lime juice and yogurt for 30 seconds. Add the chervil and seasoning and blend for a further 15 seconds.
4. Serve the sauce in a Black and Clear Jug and pour over the eggs before serving.

Serves 4

Quails' eggs are not always available or to everyone's taste. Small hens' eggs may be substituted. Allow 1 egg, cut into quarters, per person.

SMOKED HADDOCK MOUSSE PANCAKES

Preparation time : 25 minutes
Cooking time : 15 minutes
Calories per serving : 267

•

100g (4oz) skinless smoked haddock fillet
1 egg white
75ml (3fl oz) double cream
8 pancakes (page 124)
15g (¹/₂ oz) butter
2tbsp finely chopped onion
1tbsp chopped fresh tarragon (or 1tsp dried)
300ml (¹/₂ pint) chicken stock (page 126)
1tsp cornflour
1tbsp cold water
8 small sprigs of fresh tarragon for garnish

To ripen avocados quickly, put them in a brown paper bag along with a ripe banana and keep in a warm place (this also works with unripe pears and peaches).

Kitchen Duo
Ladle/Slotted Spoon
Break-resistant and dishwasher-proof, can be used not just as a ladle, but also to strain foods.

Preheat oven to 190°C (375°F/Gas Mark 5)

1. Blend the smoked haddock in a liquidiser or food processor for 1 minute until smooth. Use the Cook's Maid to separate the egg (store the egg yolk in the fridge for use in another recipe). Add the egg white and blend for a further 30 seconds. Add the cream and blend for 30 seconds until smooth and creamy.
2. Place a tablespoonful of fish mixture in the centre of a pancake, fold to form a neat parcel and place in a buttered ovenproof dish. Repeat with the remaining pancakes and bake uncovered for 15 minutes.
3. Melt the butter in a small pan and gently fry the onions until soft. Add the tarragon and stock, and then boil rapidly until the liquid has been reduced by a third. Mix the cornflour with the water in a Tropical Serving Cup and add to the sauce, stirring until slightly thickened.
4. To serve, pour a little sauce on to four warm plates and place 2 fish parcels in the centre of each. Garnish with a sprig of tarragon.

Serves 4

Try using other types of smoked fish instead of haddock. For very special occasions, splash out with smoked salmon.

Serve on a bed of oak leaf lettuce. The distinctive flavour of the lettuce sets off the flavour of the fish, and the leaves add a touch of colour.

Remove eggs from the refrigerator one hour before use. Cold eggs don't beat easily and yolks tend to burst.

An easy way to skin tomatoes is to put them in boiling water for about 20 seconds (first making a small incision in the skin), then into iced water.

EGG COCOTTES JARDINIÈRE

Preparation time : 15 minutes
Cooking time : 40 minutes
Calories per serving : 150

•

25g (1oz) butter
1tbsp finely chopped onion
1/2 red pepper, diced
1/2 green pepper, diced
1 small courgette, diced
1 small carrot, diced
salt and freshly ground black pepper
4 eggs
1tbsp chopped fresh parsley for garnish

1. Melt the butter in a frying pan, add the prepared vegetables and fry gently over a medium heat for 5 minutes without browning. Add salt and pepper to taste.
2. Divide the mixture between 4 Tropical Serving Cups. Gently crack an egg over each cupful of vegetables, taking care not to break the yolks, and then seal the Cups.
3. Adjust the grid of the Space Saver Crisper to sit halfway in the container. Place the Serving Cups on to the grid and pour boiling water down the side of the Crisper until it reaches three quarters of the way up the Serving Cups. Seal and leave to stand for 30 minutes. Don't overcook the eggs - the yolks should be runny.
4. Serve garnished with chopped parsley.

Serves 4

Eat with hot crusty wholemeal bread or rolls.

BEAN AND PASTA SOUP

Preparation time : 15 minutes
Cooking time : 35 minutes
Calories per serving : 140

•

1tbsp olive oil
1 small onion, diced
2 cloves garlic, finely chopped
1 medium carrot, diced
1 stick celery, sliced
100g (4oz) ham, cut into 1cm (1/2 in) cubes
100g (4oz) canned flageolet beans
100g (4oz) canned cannellini beans
600ml (1 pint) chicken stock (page 126)
4 medium tomatoes, skinned, seeded and finely chopped
25g (1oz) egg vermicelli, crushed
salt and freshly ground black pepper
1tbsp chopped fresh marjoram (or 1tsp dried)
1tbsp chopped fresh oregano (or 1tsp dried)

1. Heat the oil in a large saucepan and fry the onion, garlic, carrot and celery over a low heat for 5 minutes, stirring with a Kitchen Duo Spoon to prevent browning. Add the ham and cook for a further 5 minutes.

TOP *Bean & Pasta Soup* BOTTOM *Egg Cocottes Jardinière*

17

TOP *Chestnut Pâté* CENTRE *Leek & Apple Soup* BOTTOM *Spicy Tofu Soup*

18

2. Add the beans and stock, bring to the boil, cover and simmer for 20 minutes.

3. Add the tomatoes and vermicelli and leave to cook for a further 5 minutes. Adjust seasoning and add the herbs just before serving.

Serves 4

Do not add the vermicelli more than 5 minutes before eating as they swell up and thicken the soup too much.

CHESTNUT PÂTÉ

Preparation time : 10 minutes plus overnight soaking
Cooking time : 40 minutes plus 2 hours chilling
Calories per serving : 90-135

·

100g (4oz) dried chestnuts, soaked overnight
300ml (1/2 pint) vegetable stock (page 126)
1tbsp olive oil
1/2 medium onion, chopped
2 cloves garlic, finely chopped
100g (4oz) parsnip, diced
50g (2oz) mushrooms, sliced
1tsp chopped fresh thyme (or 1/4 tsp dried)
1tbsp brandy
salt and freshly ground black pepper

1. Place the chestnuts and stock in a saucepan and bring to the boil. Cover and simmer for 30 minutes.

2. Heat the oil in another saucepan, and gently fry the onion, garlic and parsnip for 5 minutes. Add the mushrooms, 75ml (5tbsp) stock from the chestnuts, thyme and brandy. Cover and cook gently for a further 15 minutes.

3. Blend the vegetables in a liquidiser or food processor for 30 seconds. Drain the chestnuts and add with the salt and pepper. Blend for a further 30 seconds, or longer for a smoother consistency.

4. Transfer the mixture into the Butter Dish; smooth over, cover and chill before serving.

Serves 4–6

This recipe uses dried chestnuts because the chestnut season is short. However, when available, use 225g (8oz) shelled, fresh chestnuts and reduce the simmering time to 15 minutes.

LEEK AND APPLE SOUP

Preparation time : 10 minutes
Cooking time : 35 minutes
Calories per serving : 180

·

25g (1oz) butter
175g (6oz) leek, cleaned and chopped
2 Granny Smith apples, cored and chopped
75g (3oz) potatoes, peeled and diced
600ml (1 pint) vegetable stock (page 126)
few strands saffron
75ml (3fl oz) double cream
salt and freshly ground black pepper
few fine rings of leek for garnish

1. Melt the butter in a saucepan, add the leek, apple and potato and fry over a low heat for 5 minutes. Add the stock and saffron and bring to the boil. Cover and simmer for 20 minutes.

2. When the soup has cooled slightly pour into a liquidiser or food processor, in 2 batches, and blend for 1 minute each time. Strain the puréed soup through the Double Colander into a 2 litre Bowl.

3. Return the soup to a clean saucepan. Adjust seasoning, add the cream and reheat before serving. Garnish with a few rings of leek.

Serves 4

This soup makes a refreshing starter served ice cold and garnished with finely chopped pieces of apple.

SPICY TOFU SOUP

Preparation time : 20 minutes
Calories per serving : 60

·

600ml (1 pint) vegetable stock (page 126)
1 small carrot, cut into matchstick-sized strips
50g (2oz) button mushrooms, finely sliced
50g (2oz) water chestnuts, finely sliced

A few grains of rice in the salt cellar will absorb moisture and keep salt free-running.

Butter Dish
Keeps butter fresher, by allowing the air to circulate around it. Can also be used to serve pâtés and terrines.

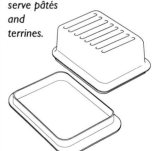

50g (2oz) bamboo shoots, cut into matchstick-
sized strips
tofu 7.5cm (3in) square
1tbsp Worcestershire sauce
1tbsp white wine vinegar
pinch chilli powder
2tbsp cornflour
2tbsp cold water
salt and freshly ground black pepper
1 egg white, lightly beaten
1tsp sesame oil
1tbsp chopped spring onion for garnish
2tsp finely chopped ginger for garnish

1. Place the vegetable stock, carrot, mushrooms, water chestnuts and bamboo shoots in a saucepan and bring to the boil. Reduce to simmer, cover and cook for 3 minutes.
2. Cut the tofu into 1cm (½ in) cubes, add to the soup and simmer for 2 more minutes.
3. In a Tropical Serving Cup mix together the Worcestershire sauce, vinegar, chilli powder, cornflour and water, and then add to the soup. Return the soup to the boil, stirring constantly using a Kitchen Duo Spoon, and cook until slightly thickened.
4. Add salt and pepper to taste and then trickle the egg white into the soup, stirring at the end. Make sure it doesn't come to the boil. Just before serving, add the sesame oil.
5. Serve in Oriental Bowls with a sprinkle of chopped spring onion and ginger.

Serves 4

OYSTER MUSHROOMS ON PASTRY CUSHIONS

Preparation time : 15 minutes
Cooking time : 20 minutes
Calories per serving : 300

175g (6oz) puff pastry
2tbsp vegetable oil
1 small onion, finely chopped
2 cloves garlic, finely chopped
1tsp finely chopped fresh ginger

225g (8oz) oyster mushrooms, sliced
1tbsp sherry
150ml (¼ pint) vegetable stock (page 126)
1tsp cornflour
1tbsp cold water
salt and freshly ground black pepper
1tbsp chopped fresh parsley

Preheat oven to 190°C (375°F/Gas Mark 5)

1. Use the Pastry Sheet and Rolling Pin to roll the pastry to just over 20cm (8in) square. Trim the edges of the pastry and cut into 4 pieces each approximately 10cm (4in) square. Fold each square in half diagonally and cut through the 2 layers parallel to and 1cm (½ in) from the open edges, but stopping 2cm (¾ in) from the centre point.
2. Unfold the pastry, brush a little water along the cut strips, lift one cut point of the strip over to the opposite inner point and press down. Repeat with the other strip. Place the cases on to a baking tray and bake for 15-20 minutes until golden brown. Press the centre down to form a deep well; leave to cool.
3. Heat the oil in a pan, add the onion, garlic and ginger and fry for 2 minutes. Add the oyster mushrooms and sherry and fry for a further 3 minutes over a medium heat. Add the stock and bring to the boil. Reduce the heat, cover and cook gently for 10 minutes.
4. Mix the cornflour and water in a Tropical Serving Cup and add to the mushroom mixture. Return to the boil, stirring until the sauce thickens. Adjust seasoning and add the chopped parsley. Mix thoroughly and divide between the pastry cases just before serving.

Serves 4

One large pastry case may be made instead of individual cushions. You will need to extend the baking time to 30-35 minutes, until golden brown.

Tupperware came to the UK and Ireland in 1960. It was an immediate success, its informal parties offering housewives a much needed social occasion as well as a new job opportunity. Today there are 10,000 demonstrators, 800 managers and 62 distributors serving the market.

Oriental Bowls
For rice, noodles, soups, stir-fries or pasta. The covers of these bowls keep food hot at the table or can be used as extra plates for accompaniments.

Oyster Mushrooms on Pastry Cushions

2
Fig. *Fish*

It's better to buy frozen fish rather than fresh that has been stored too long.

When skinning a fish fillet, dip your fingertips in salt to get a better grip on the skin. You can get the smell off your hands by washing them with soap and mustard powder.

COLD SALMON WITH WATERCRESS SAUCE

Preparation time : 5 minutes
Cooking time : 2-3 hours
Calories per serving : 338

•

1 bouquet garni
1 medium onion, sliced
1 carrot, sliced
1/2 tsp salt and 10 peppercorns
1.5 litres (2½ pints) cold water
4 salmon steaks, 175g-225g (6oz-8oz) each
1 bunch watercress, trimmed
150ml (¼ pint) plain yogurt
2tbsp fresh orange juice
salt and freshly ground black pepper
1 lemon, sliced for garnish

1. Place the bouquet garni, onion, carrot, salt, peppercorns and cold water in a saucepan and bring to the boil.
2. Pour the boiling water mixture into the bowl of the Multi-Server. Place the salmon steaks in the colander and lower into the bowl. Cover and leave undisturbed until cold: 2-3 hours. (Leaving the salmon in the Multi-Server with the poaching liquid until cold prevents the fish going dry.)
3. Blend the watercress, yogurt, and orange juice in a liquidiser or food processor for 1 minute. Add salt and pepper to taste and blend for a further 15 seconds.
4. To serve, transfer the salmon on to a serving plate and pour the watercress sauce over. Garnish with lemon slices.

Serves 4

RED MULLET PROVENÇAL

Preparation time : 20 minutes
Cooking time : 40 minutes
Calories per serving : 345

•

2tbsp olive oil
3 cloves garlic, finely chopped
1 medium onion, sliced
450g (1lb) tomatoes, skinned, seeded and chopped
1tbsp tomato purée
2tbsp coarsely chopped fresh basil
150ml (¼ pint) dry white wine
1tbsp cornflour
1tbsp water
salt and freshly ground black pepper
4 red mullet, about 225g (8oz) each, cleaned
1tbsp chopped fresh basil for garnish

Preheat oven to 190°C (375°F/Gas Mark 5)

1. Heat the olive oil and fry the garlic and onion for 5 minutes over a medium heat until starting to brown.
2. Add the tomatoes, tomato purée, basil and white wine and bring to the boil. Mix the cornflour and water together and add to the pan; cook, stirring with a Kitchen Duo Spoon until thickened. Add salt and pepper to taste.
3. Place the red mullet in an ovenproof dish and pour the tomato sauce over. Cover with foil and bake for 30 minutes. Sprinkle with chopped basil before serving.

Serves 4

Prawns are also delicious with this sauce. Simply add 450g (1lb) prawns once the sauce has thickened, and continue cooking until the prawns are heated through.

THAI FISH PARCELS

Preparation time : 20 minutes
Cooking time : 30 minutes
Calories per serving : 300

•

1tbsp olive oil
1 small onion, finely chopped
100g (4oz) button mushrooms, sliced
1 small red pepper, diced
100g (4oz) Kenyan green beans, cut into 2.5cm (1in) pieces
25g (1oz) bulgar wheat
salt and freshly ground black pepper
350g (12oz) salmon fillet, skinned
350g (12oz) sole fillet, skinned
2 sticks lemon grass, cut in half

1. Heat the oil in a saucepan and fry the onion, mushrooms, pepper and beans over a medium heat for 5 minutes without browning. Add the bulgar wheat, salt and pepper and cook for a further minute.
2. Cut the salmon and sole into 1cm (½ in) wide strips and crush the lemon grass.

TOP LEFT *Red Mullet Provençal* TOP RIGHT *Cold Salmon with Watercress Sauce* BOTTOM *Thai Fish Parcels*

TOP *Quick Fish Quenelles* BOTTOM *Chinese-Style Poached Trout*

3. Divide the vegetables, fish and lemon grass between four sheets of foil. Fold in half, and fold the edges over several times (firmly) to seal the mixture.

4. Place the parcels on the grid in the Space Saver Crisper and pour boiling water down the side of the Crisper, to the halfway level. Seal and leave for 30 minutes.

5. Serve 1 parcel per person. Allow each to open their own parcel, to enjoy the aroma of the contents.

Serves 4

Extra care should be taken not to split the foil when folding, as water will enter the parcel and spoil the flavour of the fish.

CHINESE-STYLE POACHED TROUT

Preparation time : 10 minutes
Cooking time : 25 minutes
Calories per serving : 156-312

•

2 small trout, about 225g (8oz) each, cleaned
¼ lime, sliced
1tsp salt
2tbsp vegetable oil
1 clove garlic, crushed
2.5cm (1in) cube fresh ginger, finely shredded
3 spring onions, finely shredded
2tbsp dark soy sauce
1tsp sesame oil

1. Place the trout on the grid in the Space Saver Crisper, removing the heads if the fish are too long. Add the lime slices and salt.

2. Pour boiling water in at the side to cover the fish, seal and leave for 25 minutes. Lift out the grid to drain the trout and transfer to a warm serving plate.

3. Heat the oil, add the garlic and fry for 1 minute over a high heat. Discard the garlic, add the ginger and spring onions and continue to cook for 30 seconds. Pour the hot oil and vegetable mixture over the fish, taking care as it will sizzle.

4. Add the soy sauce and sesame oil, and serve immediately.

Serves 2, or 4 if used as part of a Chinese main meal

Sea Bass makes an excellent (if expensive) alternative.

QUICK FISH QUENELLES

Preparation time : 15 minutes
Chilling time : 1 hour
Cooking time : 20 minutes
Calories per serving : 425

•

175g (6oz) whiting, flesh only
175g (6oz) turbot, flesh only
2 egg whites, lightly beaten
75ml (3fl oz) double cream
75g (3oz) shelled prawns, chopped
50g (2oz) shelled pistachio nuts, chopped
1tbsp chopped fresh chives (or 1tsp dried)
1tsp salt and ¼tsp freshly ground black pepper
15g (½oz) plain flour
300ml (½ pint) milk
100g (4oz) Cheddar cheese, grated

1. Blend the whiting and turbot in a liquidiser or food processor for 2 minutes until smooth. Gradually blend in the egg whites and then the cream. Transfer the mixture to a 2 litre Bowl, seal and refrigerate for 1 hour.

2. After refrigeration, mix in the prawns, pistachio nuts, chives and seasoning. Form the mixture into 12 egg-shaped quenelles and place them on the grid in the Space Saver Crisper. Gently pour boiling water in at the side, not directly on to the quenelles, until they are well covered. Seal and leave for 10 minutes.

3. Place the flour, milk and half of the cheese in the Quick Shake, shake well and pour into a saucepan. Bring to the boil over a medium heat, stirring constantly.

4. Drain and transfer the quenelles to a shallow ovenproof dish. Pour the cheese sauce over, sprinkle with the remaining cheese and grill under a high heat until brown. Serve immediately, while the sauce is still bubbling.

Serves 4

A really fresh fish has a very slippery shiny skin, bulging bright eyes, bright pink or reddish gills and is hard to grip. If the scales are coming off and it doesn't have a pleasant smell - don't buy it!

Space Saver Crisper
Abundant fresh vegetables, fruits and salads can be stored in the six litre capacity. A clever freshness grid lifts produce away from fridge condensation, to ensure extra crispness.

SMOKED HADDOCK FLAN

Preparation time : 25 minutes
Cooking time : 20 minutes
Calories per serving : 445

•

300ml (¹/₂ pint) milk
1 bouquet garni
1 medium onion, chopped
10 peppercorns
225g (8oz) smoked haddock
1 quantity shortcrust pastry (page 124)
25g (1oz) plain flour
25g (1oz) butter
2 hard-boiled eggs, chopped
2tbsp chopped fresh dill (or 2tsp dried)
15g (¹/₂oz) fresh breadcrumbs
15g (¹/₂oz) Cheddar cheese, grated

Preheat oven to 190°C (375°F/Gas Mark 5)

1. Place the milk, bouquet garni, half the onion and all the peppercorns in a saucepan and bring to the boil. Add the smoked haddock and return to the boil. Pour into the Multi-Server, cover and leave for 15 minutes.
2. Using the Rolling Pin and Pastry Sheet, roll out the pastry and use to line a 20cm (8in) flan ring. Bake blind (page 124).
3. When the fish is cooked, strain the liquid into the Quick Shake, add the flour and shake to blend thoroughly. Melt the butter over a low heat and fry the remaining onion for 5 minutes. Pour in the flour and milk mixture and bring to the boil, stirring constantly.
4. Flake the fish and add to the sauce with the chopped egg and dill. Gently mix together and pour into the flan case. Mix the breadcrumbs and cheese together and sprinkle over the flan. Bake for 15 minutes.

Serves 4

PLAICE, ASPARAGUS AND SAFFRON TWISTS

Preparation time : 15 minutes
Cooking time : 20 minutes
Calories per serving : 300

•

4 plaice, about 225g (8oz) each, skinned and filleted
salt and freshly ground black pepper
100g (4oz) fine asparagus, blanched
large sprig of parsley
25g (1oz) plain flour
300ml (¹/₂ pint) fish stock (page 126)
100ml (4fl oz) white wine
25g (1oz) butter
few strands of saffron

1. Sprinkle salt and pepper on each plaice fillet. Trim and cut each asparagus in half, and divide between the fillets. Roll the plaice around the asparagus, starting at the wide end of the fillet.
2. Transfer the plaice twists on to the grid in the Space Saver Crisper, add the parsley and pour boiling water down the side until the twists are totally covered. Add 1tsp salt, seal and leave for 20 minutes.
3. Put the flour, fish stock and wine into the Quick Shake and shake well. Pour into a saucepan, add the butter and saffron and bring to the boil, stirring constantly. Cover and simmer gently for 15 minutes.
4. Lift out grid to drain, and transfer the fish on to individual plates. Season the sauce to taste and spoon over the fish.

Serves 4

Other flat fish such as Dover or lemon sole can also be served in this way.

MACKEREL WITH HERB AND LEMON STUFFING

Preparation time : 20 minutes
Cooking time : 35 minutes
Calories per serving : 500

•

1 lemon
1tbsp vegetable oil
¹/₂ medium onion, chopped
50g (2oz) fresh breadcrumbs
2tsp chopped fresh rosemary (or 1tsp dried)
2tsp chopped fresh thyme (or 1tsp dried)
1tbsp chopped fresh parsley (or 1tsp dried)
¹/₂ tsp salt and freshly ground black pepper
2 mackerel, about 275g (10oz) each, gutted, boned and kept whole
lemon wedges and fresh herbs for garnish

A cracked flan case can be made leakproof by sealing with a little egg white and briefly re-baking.

Quick Shake
Saves energy and saves spillage. For mixing those healthy fruit drinks and fresh salad dressings. Will also mix eggs, and whip cream simply and quickly.

TOP *Mackerel with Herb & Lemon Stuffing* CENTRE *Plaice, Asparagus & Saffron Twists* BOTTOM *Smoked Haddock Flan*

TOP *Cod Steaks Mediterranean* BOTTOM *Cod & Prawn Patties*

1. Using the Cook's Maid, remove the zest and juice of the lemon. Heat the oil and gently fry the onion for 5 minutes without browning. Add the lemon juice and zest, breadcrumbs, herbs, salt and pepper, and mix thoroughly.

2. Remove the heads and pat the mackerel dry. Divide the stuffing between the fish and place inside the body cavity.

3. Wrap each fish in a sheet of foil. Fold the edges several times to seal the parcels. Place on the grid in the Space Saver Crisper, and pour in boiling water until the fish are totally immersed. Seal and leave for 25 minutes.

4. Remove the foil before serving and garnish with lemon wedges and small sprigs of herbs.

Serves 2

COD STEAKS MEDITERRANEAN

Preparation time : 15 minutes
Cooking time : 40 minutes
Calories per serving : 280

•

2tbsp flour
4 cod steaks, 175g-225g (6oz-8oz) each
2tbsp olive oil
1 medium onion, sliced
2 cloves garlic, finely chopped
1 small red pepper, sliced
1 small green pepper, sliced
4 large tomatoes, skinned and chopped
20 black olives
1 bouquet garni
150ml (¼ pint) red wine
salt and freshly ground black pepper
1tbsp cornflour
1tbsp water
1tbsp chopped fresh parsley for garnish

1. Using the Sift n Stor, lightly sprinkle flour on to both sides of the cod steaks. Preheat the oil in a large lidded frying pan and fry the steaks quickly on both sides to seal in the juices, turning with a Server/Wide Spatula. Remove the fish from the pan and reduce the heat.

2. Gently fry the onion, garlic and peppers for 5 minutes, stirring with the Wide Spatula. Add the tomatoes, olives and bouquet garni, and mix well.

3. Return the fish to the pan, add the wine and bring to the boil. Reduce the heat, cover and gently simmer for 25 minutes.

4. Transfer the fish to a warm serving dish, remove the bouquet garni, and adjust the seasoning. Mix the cornflour and water together, add to the pan and return to the boil, stirring constantly until the sauce has thickened slightly.

5. To serve, spoon the sauce around the fish and sprinkle with chopped parsley.

Serves 4

COD AND PRAWN PATTIES

Preparation time : 20 minutes
Chilling time : 1 hour
Cooking time : 30 minutes
Calories per serving : 350

•

450g (1lb) boiled potatoes
1 egg plus 1 egg yolk
1tbsp chopped fresh tarragon (or 1tsp dried)
salt and freshly ground black pepper
350g (12oz) cod fillet, cooked
100g (4oz) peeled prawns, chopped
50g (2oz) fresh breadcrumbs
4tbsp vegetable oil for frying

1. Mash the potatoes and push through a sieve to remove all the lumps. Add the two egg yolks (use the Cook's Maid to separate), plus tarragon and seasoning. Mix thoroughly. Flake the fish and add with the prawns to the potato mixture.

2. Use the Hamburger Press to make into 8 burger shapes and freeze for 2 hours.

3. Lightly beat the egg white, brush over the chilled fish cakes and then coat each one with breadcrumbs.

4. Fry the fish cakes in the oil over a medium heat for about 5 minutes each side, until golden brown.

Serves 4

Other types of cooked white fish may also be used as an alternative to cod.

Fish

All oils are best kept in a cool, dark place - ideally a larder. Your bottle of best extra-virgin olive oil may look attractive left out in the kitchen, but it will quickly go rancid.

Sift n Stor
Instead of measuring and sifting separately, do it all in one operation and save time with the handy Sift n Stor.

CASSEROLE DE MER

Preparation time : 15 minutes
Cooking time : 35 minutes
Calories per serving : 340

•

1tbsp vegetable oil
1 medium onion, sliced
3 cloves garlic, finely chopped
1tbsp tomato purée
2 large tomatoes, skinned, seeded and chopped
1 leek, cut into 1cm (¹/₂in) slices
450ml (³/₄ pint) fish stock (page 126)
150ml (¹/₄ pint) white wine
1 sprig fresh thyme (or 1tsp dried)
1 large sprig rosemary, chopped (or 2tsp dried)
2 bay leaves
225g (8oz) monkfish
225g (8oz) turbot fillet
225g (8oz) red mullet fillet
225g (8oz) uncooked prawns in shell
20 mussels, thoroughly cleaned
1tbsp chopped parsley for garnish

It's an old French tradition that whoever finds a bay leaf in their meal has to make love to the cook or chef.

The smell and taste of fish often remains on cooking utensils, plates and cutlery. To get rid of it, wash them in water to which a little vinegar has been added.

1. Heat the oil in a large saucepan and gently fry the onion and garlic for 3 minutes. Add the tomato purée, chopped tomatoes and leek, and fry for a further 2 minutes. Add the stock, wine, thyme, rosemary and bay leaves, and bring to the boil. Reduce the heat, cover and simmer for 15 minutes.
2. Cut the monkfish, turbot and red mullet into large chunks. Add the monkfish to the liquid and cook for 5 minutes; add the remainder of the fish chunks along with the prawns and mussels, and bring to the boil. Reduce heat and simmer for a further 10 minutes.
3. Remove the thyme and bay leaves, and adjust seasoning to taste. Using a Kitchen Duo Slotted Spoon, divide the fish mixture between 4 soup plates. Then with the Ladle, pour the soup over the fish. Sprinkle with chopped parsley.

Serves 4

PLAICE FILLETS IN MUSHROOM CUPS

Preparation time : 15 minutes
Cooking time : 25 minutes
Calories per serving : 295

•

225g (8oz) cooked spinach (frozen or fresh), squeezed dry and chopped
2tbsp fromage frais
large pinch ground cinnamon
salt and freshly ground black pepper
8 plaice fillets, about 100g (4oz) each, skinned
150ml (¹/₄ pint) white wine
8 open-capped mushrooms
1tbsp melted butter
15g (¹/₂oz) flour
¹/₂tsp mustard powder
1tbsp tomato purée
150ml (¹/₄ pint) milk
15g (¹/₂oz) butter
1 tomato, skinned, seeded and chopped
1tbsp chopped fresh parsley for garnish

Preheat oven to 190°C (375°F/Gas Mark 5)

1. Thoroughly mix the spinach, fromage frais, cinnamon and seasoning, and spread on to the plaice fillets, skinned side up. Fold the fillets in half lengthwise and carefully roll up, starting at the wider end.
2. Place in a deep ovenproof dish, add the wine, cover with foil and bake for 20 minutes until cooked.
3. Toss the mushrooms in the melted butter and grill under a medium heat for 10 minutes, turning once.
4. Put the flour, mustard powder, tomato purée and milk into the Quick Shake and shake to blend. Pour into a saucepan, add the butter and bring to the boil, stirring constantly. Add the chopped tomato and any liquid from the cooked fish. Adjust seasoning and cook for 2 minutes.
5. To serve, put a plaice roll on each mushroom, spoon the sauce over and sprinkle with a little chopped parsley.

Serves 4

TOP *Plaice Fillets in Mushroom Cups* BOTTOM *Casserole de Mer*

3
Main Meals

Use the Ice Cube Set to freeze tomato purée, which goes mouldy quickly. When frozen, pack in a 0.4 litre Freeze n Stor and add one or two wedges to sauces and casseroles as required.

Thin-skinned citrus fruit are the juiciest.

CHICKEN CURRY WITH OKRA

Preparation time : 15 minutes
Cooking time : 35 minutes
Calories per serving : 295

•

450g (1lb) boned chicken meat
2tbsp vegetable oil
225g (8oz) okra (ladies' fingers)
1 medium onion, grated
2 cloves garlic, finely chopped
1tsp cumin seeds
1tsp ground coriander
$^{1}/_{2}$ tsp turmeric
$^{1}/_{2}$ tsp crushed dried red chilli
1tbsp grated fresh ginger
2tbsp tomato purée
2tbsp flour
450ml ($^{3}/_{4}$ pint) chicken stock (page 126)
2tbsp chopped fresh coriander

1. Cut the chicken into large chunks. Heat the oil in a pan over a high heat and quickly fry the chicken to seal in the juices, turning the pieces with the Kitchen Duo Spoon. Remove from the pan. Fry the okra until just turning brown and set aside, with the chicken.
2. Fry the onion, garlic, cumin seeds, ground coriander, turmeric, chilli and ginger for 1 minute. Add the tomato purée and flour and cook for a further 2 minutes. Add the stock a little at a time, stirring to prevent any lumps forming, and then bring to the boil.
3. Return the chicken and okra to the pan, bring to the boil again, then cover and simmer gently for 20 minutes. Add the chopped coriander and adjust seasoning to taste before serving.

Serves 4

5-SPICE DUCK WITH PLUM SAUCE

Preparation time : 10 minutes
Marinating time : 12 hours or overnight
Cooking time : 20 minutes
Calories per serving : 640

•

2tsp 5-spice powder
$^{1}/_{2}$ tsp salt

$^{1}/_{4}$ tsp ground white pepper
1tsp brandy
4 large duck breast fillets, about 175g (6oz) each
450g (1lb) red plums or one 439g (15oz) can of red plums
2tbsp cold water
25g (1oz) soft brown sugar
1tbsp red wine vinegar
1 spring onion, finely shredded for garnish

Preheat oven to 200°C (400°F/Gas Mark 6)

1. Mix together the 5-spice powder, salt, white pepper and brandy in a 3 litre Bowl, and rub well into the duck. Leave to marinate uncovered, skin side up.
2. Stone the plums and cut into quarters. Place in a saucepan with the water and simmer for 5 minutes. Add the sugar and vinegar and cook for a further 5 minutes. (With tinned plums reduce to 3 minutes.)
3. Place the duck fillets, skin side up, on a rack inside a roasting pan and roast for 20 minutes. (Do not open oven door whilst cooking.)
4. To serve, let the duck stand for a few minutes, then cut diagonally into slices. Pour hot plum sauce around each portion and garnish with spring onion.

Serves 4

After rubbing the duck with the spice mixture, allow the skin to dry out as much as possible before cooking, so that it crisps nicely in the oven.

CHICKEN IN LEMON AND LIME

Preparation time : 15 minutes
Cooking time : 35 minutes
Calories per serving : 455

•

1tbsp sesame oil
1tbsp sherry
$^{1}/_{2}$ tsp salt and large pinch of white pepper
3tbsp cornflour
4 skinless chicken breast fillets, about 175g (6oz) each
1 lemon
1 lime
300ml ($^{1}/_{2}$ pint) chicken stock (page 126)
40g ($1^{1}/_{2}$ oz) caster sugar

TOP *5-Spice Duck with Plum Sauce* CENTRE *Chicken in Lemon & Lime* BOTTOM *Chicken Curry with Okra*

TOP *Normandy Pork* BOTTOM *Vegetable Couscous*

1tbsp cold water
2tbsp vegetable oil
4 slices each of lemon and lime

1. In a 2 litre Bowl mix together the sesame oil, sherry, salt, pepper and 2tbsp cornflour. Add the chicken fillets, each cut into 2 thin slices.

2. Using the Cook's Maid, remove the zest and juice from the lemon and lime and place in a saucepan. Add the stock and sugar and bring to the boil. Mix the rest of the cornflour and water together and add to the saucepan, stirring constantly until the sauce thickens. Cover and remove from heat.

3. Heat the oil in a pan and fry the chicken slices over a medium heat for 8 minutes each side, until golden brown and cooked through. Place on a serving dish and keep warm.

4. To serve, add the lemon and lime slices to the sauce and reheat. Adjust seasoning and pour over the chicken.

Serves 4

If fresh limes are not available, then 75ml (5tbsp) lime juice cordial can be used instead.

NORMANDY PORK

Preparation time : 20 minutes
Cooking time : 1 hour 5 minutes
Calories per serving : 690

·

700g (1¹/₂lb) boneless pork steaks
2tbsp flour
3tbsp vegetable oil
1 medium onion, sliced
2 sticks celery, cut into small pieces
2 Bramley apples, peeled, cored and sliced
4tbsp calvados
300ml (¹/₂ pint) vegetable stock (page 126)
1 Granny Smith apple, cored and sliced (for garnish)
25g (1oz) butter
salt and freshly ground black pepper
2tbsp chopped fresh parsley

1. Trim and cut the pork into 2.5cm (1in) cubes, place in a 2 litre Bowl and coat in the flour. Heat 2tbsp of the oil in a saucepan and, when hot, fry the pork (a few cubes at a time) until brown, to seal in the juices. Remove and keep warm until all the pork has been sealed.

2. Add the remaining oil and gently fry the onion, celery and apples for 5 minutes. Return the pork to the saucepan and add the calvados. Cook for a further 2 minutes. Add the stock, bring to the boil, then cover and simmer for 45 minutes.

3. Fry the sliced Granny Smith apple in the butter until brown.

4. When the pork is cooked, adjust seasoning and stir in the chopped parsley. Transfer to a warm serving plate and garnish with fried apple slices.

Serves 4

You can substitute brandy for calvados.

VEGETABLE COUSCOUS

Preparation time : 20 minutes
Cooking time : 25 minutes
Calories per serving : 460

·

225g (8oz) aubergine
salt
2tbsp olive oil
1 medium onion, cut into thin wedges
1 red pepper, cut into long strips
2 sticks celery, cut into 1cm (¹/₂ in) slices
2 medium courgettes, cut into 2.5cm (1in) chunks
100g (4oz) baby cobs of corn, cut into 2.5cm (1in) pieces
one 397g (14oz) can creamed sweetcorn
300ml (¹/₂ pint) vegetable stock (page 126)
275g (10oz) couscous
1tbsp chopped fresh parsley

1. Cut the aubergine into 2.5cm (1in) chunks, sprinkle liberally with salt, and set aside for about 15 minutes.

2. Heat the oil in a large saucepan and gently fry the onions for 5 minutes. Rinse off the aubergine and add to the pan with the rest of the vegetables. Cook for a further 5 minutes. Add the creamed sweetcorn and stock, and bring to the boil. Cover and simmer for 20 minutes.

Keep fresh parsley (or any other herbs) ready chopped in a Tupperware container in the freezer. It doesn't need to be thawed before being added to cooked dishes or sprinkled over food as a garnish.

2 litre Bowl
A very useful size for keeping perishable foods and salads in the fridge. The unique Tupperware airtight seal ensures that food keeps fresher longer.

3. In another saucepan, add the couscous and 1tsp salt to 1 litre of boiling water and return to the boil. Transfer to the Multi-Server, cover and leave undisturbed for 15 minutes.

4. Adjust the seasoning to the vegetable mixture, add the chopped parsley and serve with the couscous.

Serves 4

CARPET BAG TURKEY

Preparation time : 10 minutes
Cooking time : 30 minutes
Calories per serving : 320

·

75g (3oz) smoked streaky bacon, cut into pieces
1 egg white
25g (1oz) mushrooms
2tbsp double cream
4 turkey breast fillets, about 150g (5oz) each
salt and freshly ground black pepper
25g (1oz) butter
2tbsp finely chopped onion
50g (2oz) button mushrooms, finely sliced
1tsp brandy
2tbsp chopped fresh chervil (or 2tsp dried)
450ml (³/₄ pint) chicken stock (page 126)
1tbsp cornflour
1tbsp cold water
4 sprigs of fresh chervil for garnish

Preheat oven to 200°C (400°F/Gas Mark 6)

1. Blend the bacon in a liquidiser or food processor for 1 minute. Add the egg white and blend for a further 30 seconds. Add the mushrooms and cream and blend for 30 seconds, until smooth.

2. Slightly flatten each turkey fillet using the palm of your hand, then make an incision in each fillet to form a pocket. Sprinkle a little salt and pepper inside and fill with the bacon mixture. Press the opening together to seal.

3. Melt the butter in a pan and when hot quickly fry both sides of the turkey slices to seal in the juices, turning with the Server/Wide Spatula. Place in an ovenproof dish, cover tightly with foil and bake for 25 minutes.

4. Place the onion and mushrooms in the pan and gently fry for 2 minutes. Add the

brandy and cook for 30 seconds. Add the chopped chervil and stock, increase the heat and boil rapidly for 2 minutes. Mix the cornflour and water together and add to the pan. Cook, stirring until sauce thickens.

5. To serve, spoon the sauce over the turkey and garnish with sprigs of chervil.

Serves 4

If small turkey fillets are not available, chicken breasts will work equally well.

LAMB EN CROÛTE

Preparation time : 15 minutes
Cooking time : 15 minutes
Calories per serving : 735

·

¹/₂ medium onion, finely chopped
1tbsp vegetable oil
75g (3oz) dried apricots, chopped
25g (1oz) fresh breadcrumbs
1tbsp chopped fresh rosemary (or 1tsp dried)
salt and freshly ground black pepper
225g (8oz) puff pastry
4 lean, thick-cut lamb cutlets, about
175g (6oz) each
1 egg, lightly shaken in the Quick Shake

Preheat oven to 220°C (425°F/Gas Mark 7)

1. Gently fry the onion in the oil for 5 minutes and remove from the heat. Add the apricots, breadcrumbs, rosemary and seasoning, and stir thoroughly.

2. Using the Rolling Pin and Pastry Sheet, roll out the pastry to approximately 40cm x 40cm (16in x 16in). Trim and divide into 4 equal squares.

3. Place a cutlet on top of each piece of pastry and divide the apricot mixture between them. Moisten the edges and fold over to seal, 'knocking' the edges together with the back of a knife. Decorate with pastry trimmings, brush the pastry with the egg and bake for 15 minutes until golden brown.

Serves 4

The turkey was first introduced to this country from the Americas in the 16th century. It soon became a favourite and ousted the swan as the number one festive bird on the tables of the nobility.

To substitute yoghurt for cream in cooked dishes: first stabilise it by mixing 1tsp of cornflour with a little cold water, per small carton of plain yoghurt; then cook gently for 10 minutes, stirring constantly. This will prevent it from separating.

TOP *Lamb en Croûte* BOTTOM *Carpet Bag Turkey*

TOP *Beef with Port & Lemon* CENTRE *Mixed Meat Hot Pot* BOTTOM *Pork with Ginger & Spring Onions*

PORK WITH GINGER AND SPRING ONIONS

Preparation time : 15 minutes
Cooking time : 10 minutes
Calories per serving : 303

350g (12oz) pork fillet
1cm (1/2 in) fresh ginger
4 spring onions
2tbsp vegetable oil
1tsp brandy
1tbsp oyster-flavoured sauce
1tbsp cold water

1. Cut the pork into 5mm (1/4 in) slices; finely slice the ginger and cut the spring onions into 5cm (2in) pieces.
2. Heat the oil until very hot and add the pork slices. Stir-fry quickly for about 5 minutes, turning with the Kitchen Duo Spoon until the pork is slightly brown on both sides. Add the spring onions, ginger and brandy and fry for 2 minutes, tossing and stirring constantly.
3. Add the oyster-flavoured sauce and water and continue frying for 1 minute. Serve immediately.

Serves 2, or 4 as part of a Chinese main meal

Prawns or other types of meat can be cooked in the same way and are equally delicious.

BEEF WITH PORT AND LEMON

Preparation time : 25 minutes
Cooking time : 2 hours 15 minutes
Calories per serving : 495

700g (1 1/2 lb) lean braising steak,
cut into 4cm (1 1/2 in) cubes
2tbsp flour
3tbsp vegetable oil
225g (8oz) baby onions
3 cloves garlic, finely chopped
100g (4oz) button mushrooms
1 lemon
150ml (1/4 pint) meat stock (page 126)
300ml (1/2 pint) port
2 bay leaves

large sprig of thyme
salt and freshly ground black pepper
1tbsp chopped fresh parsley

1. Coat the meat with the flour. Heat 2tbsp of the oil until hot and quickly fry the beef, in 2 batches, to seal in the juices. Transfer to a 2 litre Bowl.
2. Add the remainder of the oil and fry the onions and garlic for 3 minutes, until just starting to brown; then add the mushrooms and fry for 2 minutes.
3. Use the Cook's Maid to extract the juice and zest of the lemon, and add to the pan together with the meat, stock and port. Bring to the boil. Add the bay leaves and thyme, cover and simmer for 2 hours.
4. To serve, remove the bay leaves and thyme stalk, adjust seasoning and add parsley.

Serves 4

MIXED MEAT HOT POT

Preparation time : 40 minutes (plus overnight soaking for beans)
Cooking time : 2 hours 30 minutes
Calories per serving : 471-628

350g (12oz) rindless streaky pork,
cut into chunks
350g (12oz) braising steak, cut into chunks
6 chicken drumsticks
225g (8oz) spicy pork sausages
1 medium onion, sliced
2 carrots, diced
2 sticks celery, sliced
2tbsp flour
one 397g (14oz) can chopped tomatoes
300ml (1/2 pint) vegetable stock (page 126)
150ml (1/4 pint) red wine
175g (6oz) dried flageolet beans, soaked overnight, or one 439g (15oz) can
2 bay leaves
salt and freshly ground black pepper
chopped fresh parsley for garnish

Preheat oven to 170°C (325°F/Gas Mark 3)

1. Heat a large frying pan and fry the pork without oil until lightly brown, stirring with a Kitchen Duo Slotted Spoon. Transfer to a large, lidded, ovenproof

Reduce your fat intake by skimming fat off gravy, casseroles or sauces. The best way is to lay sheets of absorbent kitchen paper on the surface, lift and discard. The fat comes away with the paper.

Cook's Maid
Typifies the versatility of Tupperware: an egg separator, a juicer and a fine grater, all in a neat jug with its own sealable cover.

casserole dish. Fry the steak in the pork fat until brown, and add to the pork. Next fry the drumsticks, and finally the sausages. Transfer them to the casserole.

2. Fry the onion, carrots and celery gently for 3 minutes. Stir in the flour and cook for 2 more minutes. Pour in the tomatoes, stock and red wine, and bring to the boil, stirring constantly.

3. Add the flageolet beans, return to the boil and cook for 10 minutes. Pour the vegetable mixture over the meat, add the bay leaves, cover and bake for 2¹⁄₂ hours. Adjust seasoning and sprinkle with chopped parsley before serving.

Serves 6-8

COUNTRY CABBAGE

Preparation time : 45 minutes
Cooking time : 30 minutes
Calories per serving : 395

12 large green cabbage leaves
2tbsp vegetable oil
350g (12oz) lean minced beef
1 medium onion, finely chopped
2 cloves garlic, finely chopped
50g (2oz) pine nuts
3tbsp tomato purée
1tbsp chopped fresh thyme (or 1tsp dried)
one 397g (14oz) can chopped tomatoes
150ml (¹⁄₄ pint) white wine
1tsp Worcestershire sauce
1tbsp chopped fresh parsley for garnish

Preheat oven to 190°C (375°F/Gas Mark 5)

1. Cut a 'V' shape at the base of each cabbage leaf to remove the hard stem. Place the leaves in the Space Saver Crisper, pour in about 1 litre of boiling water, seal and leave to steam for 20 minutes.

2. Heat half the oil in a pan until very hot, then fry the mince over a high heat for 5 minutes, stirring to break up the meat. Add half the onion and all the garlic and cook over a medium heat for 5 minutes. Add the pine nuts, tomato purée and thyme; mix thoroughly and cook for a further 3 minutes. Transfer to a 2 litre Bowl.

3. Heat the remaining tablespoon of oil and gently fry the rest of the onion for 3

minutes. Add the chopped tomatoes, wine and Worcestershire sauce and cook gently for 5 minutes. Remove from heat.

4. Place a tablespoon of meat mixture on to the rounded end of each cabbage leaf and wrap up neatly. Place them in a deep ovenproof dish, and pour the tomato sauce over the cabbage rolls. Cover tightly with foil and bake for 30 minutes. Sprinkle with parsley before serving.

Serves 4

For a meatless alternative - substitute a mixture of 150g (5oz) dry weight bulgar wheat (pre-soaked), 50g (2oz) sunflower seeds, 25g (1oz) toasted sesame seeds, 75g (3oz) sliced mushrooms and half a red pepper, diced. Cook as for the meat version.

GAMMON WITH APPLE AND ALMOND

Preparation time : 5 minutes
Cooking time : 1 hour 25 minutes
Calories per serving : 478

900g (2lb) gammon 'D' joint
1 Bramley apple
50g (2oz) ground almonds
1tsp ground cinnamon
2tbsp clear honey

Preheat oven to 180°C (350°F/Gas Mark 4)

1. Wrap the gammon joint loosely in foil and bake for 1 hour.

2. Using the Chop n Grate, grate the apple and place in a 1 litre Bowl. Add the almonds, cinnamon and honey and mix together.

3. Unwrap the partly cooked gammon, pour away the liquid and remove the rind. Press the apple and almond mixture on to the gammon, return it to the oven and bake for a further 25 minutes. Allow to cool for at least 10 minutes before carving.

Serves 4

Pulses don't keep indefinitely: last season's dried beans or peas will be better than those dried three years ago. Always buy pulses from a shop with a rapid turnover and store them in Tupperware containers to keep fresh.

Line the bottom of the grill pan with slices of stale bread. They will absorb the fat and stop any smoking that may occur if the fat overheats.

TOP *Gammon with Apple & Almond* BOTTOM *Country Cabbage*

TOP *Mushroom & Bean Pie* BOTTOM *Guinea Fowl in Mango & Brandy Sauce*

GUINEA FOWL IN MANGO AND BRANDY SAUCE

Preparation time : 25 minutes
Cooking time : 1 hour 15 minutes
Calories per serving : 360

•

*2 guinea fowl, 900g-1kg (2lb-2¼lb) each,
jointed (reserving carcasses for stock)*
1tbsp vegetable oil
16 baby onions, peeled
2 cloves garlic, finely chopped
225g (8oz) baby carrots
1 large mango, peeled and cut into chunks
6tbsp brandy
2tbsp cornflour
2tbsp cold water
2 bay leaves
salt and freshly ground black pepper
2tbsp chopped fresh parsley
1 mango, peeled and sliced for garnish

Preheat oven to 180°C (350°F/Gas Mark 4)

1. Boil the guinea fowl carcasses in 900ml (1½ pints) of water for stock (page 126).
2. Heat the oil and fry the guinea fowl joints until golden brown. Transfer to a deep, lidded, ovenproof dish.
3. Fry the onions, garlic and carrots for 5 minutes over a medium heat. Add the first mango and brandy and set alight to burn off the alcohol, stirring until the flames die.
4. Strain the stock and add 450ml (¾ pint) to the vegetables. Mix the cornflour and water together in a Tropical Serving Cup, and add to the pan. Bring to the boil, stirring constantly, and then pour over the guinea fowl. Add the bay leaves, cover and bake for 1 hour.
5. To serve, remove the bay leaves, adjust seasoning, sprinkle with parsley and garnish with slices of mango.

Serves 4

When in season, substitute the guinea fowl with a brace of pheasant for an extra special meal.

MUSHROOM AND BEAN PIE

Preparation time : 25 minutes
Cooking time : 40 minutes
Calories per serving : 394

•

50g (2oz) Cheddar cheese, grated
1tbsp chopped fresh parsley
1 quantity dry shortcrust pastry mix (page 124)
2tbsp vegetable oil
1 medium onion, chopped
2 cloves garlic, finely chopped
*225g (8oz) Kenyan green beans, cut into
4cm (1½ in) pieces*
225g (8oz) chestnut mushrooms, sliced
one 439g (15oz) can butter beans
one 397g (14oz) can chopped tomatoes
2tbsp tomato purée
salt and freshly ground black pepper

Preheat oven to 190°C (375°F/Gas Mark 5)

1. Combine the cheese and parsley with the pastry mix. Add approximately 2tbsp cold water and mix to form a dough. Place in a 2 litre Bowl, seal and refrigerate until needed.
2. Heat the oil in a saucepan and fry the onion and garlic for 3 minutes. Add the beans and mushrooms and continue frying for 5 minutes. Add the butter beans, chopped tomatoes and tomato purée, and bring to the boil. Cover and simmer for 5 minutes. Season and transfer into a 1.2 litre (2 pint) pie dish and allow to cool slightly.
3. Using the Rolling Pin and Pastry Sheet, roll out the cheese pastry to slightly larger than the pie dish. Dampen the edge of the dish and place the pastry on top, pressing down to seal around the edge. Trim off the excess pastry and use to decorate the pie crust. Make a small steam hole in the centre, and bake for 30 minutes until golden brown.

Serves 4

To stop your tears when peeling and chopping onions, keep wetting your knife under the cold tap.

In south-east Asia alone there are more than 8,000 varieties of mango.

*The smaller the squid, the
more tender it will be.*

Multi-Server

*One of the most popular
Tupperware products, the
Multi-Server combines
versatility with practicality. Its
colander insert allows you to
poach fish or make fresh
yogurt. Soft fruits can be
rinsed and stored over ice.
Vegetables can be prepared
and stored until needed.
Because it needs no hob
space, it is ideal for boating,
caravanning, camping or
anywhere with limited cooking
facilities.*

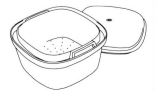

INDIAN SPICED RICE

Preparation time : 10 minutes
Cooking time : 30 minutes
Calories per serving : 272

225g (8oz) Basmati rice
2tbsp vegetable oil
1 medium onion, chopped
3 cloves garlic, finely chopped
6 whole cardamom
2tsp turmeric
2tsp ground coriander
1tsp fennel seeds
1tsp cumin seeds
2tsp poppy seeds
1/2 red pepper, thinly sliced
1 carrot, diced
75g (3oz) button mushrooms, quartered
1 courgette, sliced
150ml (1/4 pint) vegetable stock (page 126)
salt

1. Cook the rice in the Multi-Server (page 70).
2. Heat the oil in a pan and gently fry the onion and garlic for 2 minutes. Add the whole cardamom, turmeric, ground coriander, fennel, cumin and poppy seeds, and continue frying for 1 minute.
3. Add the pepper, carrot, mushrooms, courgette and stock, and bring to the boil. Reduce heat, cover and simmer for 15 minutes.
4. Add the cooked rice and salt. Stir thoroughly and cook for a further 3 minutes before serving.

Serves 4

American long grain rice may be used instead of Basmati rice.

PAELLA

Preparation time : 30 minutes
Cooking time : 35 minutes
Calories per serving : 666

225g (8oz) long grain rice
2tbsp olive oil
1 medium onion, chopped
3 cloves garlic, finely chopped
350g (12oz) chicken fillet, cubed
350g (12oz) prepared squid
1tbsp paprika
1 red pepper, sliced
50g (2oz) peas
4 large tomatoes, skinned and chopped
150ml (1/4 pint) chicken stock (page 126)
6tbsp white wine
1 large sprig fresh thyme
2 bay leaves
175g (6oz) peeled prawns
salt and freshly ground black pepper
20 mussels, cleaned thoroughly
4 Mediterranean prawns, unpeeled (optional)
3tbsp chopped fresh parsley
1 lemon, cut into wedges for garnish

1. Cook the rice in the Multi-Server (page 70).
2. In a large paella pan or frying pan, heat the oil and quickly fry the onion and garlic for 1 minute. Add the chicken and squid and fry over a high heat for 3 minutes, until the chicken starts to brown. Sprinkle the paprika over and cook for a further minute.
3. Add the pepper, peas, tomatoes, stock, wine, thyme and bay leaves and simmer uncovered over a medium heat for 10 minutes.
4. Remove the thyme stalk and bay leaves and mix in the rice and peeled prawns. Adjust seasoning and arrange the mussels and Mediterranean prawns (if you have them) on top, pushing slightly into the rice. Cook for 5 minutes until the mussels have opened and the prawns are heated through. Remember, unopened mussels should not be eaten.
5. Garnish with parsley and lemon wedges before serving straight from the pan.

Serves 4

Paella gets its name from the round, shallow, flat-bottomed, two-handled pan in which it is traditionally cooked. There are no hard and fast rules as to what should go into it - meat or fish (it is usually both) - as long as rice is one of the ingredients. In Spain the cooked paella is sometimes decorated with fresh carnations - a nice finishing touch for a dinner party or anniversary meal.

TOP *Paella* BOTTOM *Indian Spiced Rice*

45

TOP *Curried Rice & Noodles* CENTRE *Spring Vegetable Pilaff* BOTTOM *Tuna Spaghetti en Papillote*

CURRIED RICE AND NOODLES

Preparation time : 10 minutes
Cooking time : 30 minutes
Calories per serving : 423

175g (6oz) long grain rice
100g (4oz) egg vermicelli
100g (4oz) streaky bacon,
cut in 2.5cm (1in) pieces
100g (4oz) chicken fillet, cut in thin strips
1tbsp Madras curry powder
50g (2oz) frozen peas
100g (4oz) peeled prawns
4 spring onions, chopped
salt

1. Cook the rice in the Multi-Server (page 70).
2. Crush the vermicelli strands, cover with boiling water and boil for 4 minutes. Drain and reserve in a 1 litre Bowl.
3. Heat up a pan and fry the bacon for about 5 minutes, stirring until brown. Add the chicken and continue frying for a further 5 minutes.
4. Sprinkle curry powder over the meat and stir in the peas, cooked rice and vermicelli. Add the prawns and spring onions; cook until heated through. Adjust seasoning and return to the Multi-Server to serve.

Serves 4

TUNA SPAGHETTI EN PAPILLOTE

Preparation time : 20 minutes
Cooking time : 15 minutes
Calories per serving : 540

275g (10oz) spaghetti
one 397g (14oz) can tuna in brine, drained
one 100g (4oz) can smoked oysters, drained
4 large tomatoes, skinned, seeded and chopped
1 courgette, cut into short sticks
16 black olives
15g (1/2oz) capers
4tbsp coarsely chopped fresh basil
3tbsp olive oil
salt and freshly ground black pepper

Preheat oven to 190°C (375°F/Gas Mark 5)

1. Cook the spaghetti in a saucepan of boiling water for 10 minutes, drain using the Double Colander and place in a 3 litre Bowl.
2. Add the remaining ingredients and mix well with the Spoon/Draining Spoon.
3. Divide the mixture between 4 large sheets of greaseproof paper. Bring the sides of the paper together and fold several times to form a seam. Fold each of the open ends together to a point and tuck under to seal. Place the parcels on a baking sheet and bake for 15 minutes.
4. To serve, allow each person to open their own parcel, to enjoy the aroma of the contents.

Serves 4

SPRING VEGETABLE PILAFF

Preparation time : 10 minutes
Cooking time : 25 minutes
Calories per serving : 321

225g (8oz) long grain rice
1 stick lemon grass, crushed
75g (3oz) carrot
175g (6oz) broccoli
175g (6oz) baby cobs of corn
175g (6oz) mangetout peas
2tbsp olive oil
2 cloves garlic, finely chopped
6tbsp cold water
salt and freshly ground black pepper

1. Cook the rice with the lemon grass in the Multi-Server (page 70).
2. Peel and cut the carrot into thin sticks about 4cm (1 1/2 in) long. Separate the broccoli into small florets. Cut the baby corn into 2.5cm (1in) pieces. Trim and cut the peas in half.
3. Heat the oil and fry the garlic for 1 minute. Add the carrot, corn and broccoli, and stir-fry for 2 minutes. Add the peas and water. Cover and cook for 5 minutes.
4. Add the rice and seasoning, and stir thoroughly before serving.

Serves 4

Nearly 6,000 Tupperware demonstrations are held each week in the UK and Ireland, with an average attendance of eight people per party. Worldwide a demonstration takes place every 2.8 seconds.

It is said, that before her future husband will marry her, a Japanese bride-to-be must demonstrate that she can cook a perfect bowl of rice.

CANNELLONI WITH RICOTTA

Preparation time : 25 minutes
Cooking time : 20 minutes
Calories per serving : 560

175g (6oz) leeks, coarsely chopped
225g (8oz) peeled prawns
400g (14oz) Ricotta cheese
salt and freshly ground black pepper
16 easy-cook cannelloni
1tbsp vegetable oil
1 medium onion, chopped
2 cloves garlic, finely chopped
one 397g (14oz) can chopped tomatoes
300ml (¹/₂ pint) white wine
1tbsp caster sugar
1tbsp cornflour
1tbsp cold water
2tbsp chopped fresh basil (or 2tsp dried)
50g (2oz) Cheddar cheese, grated

Preheat oven to 190°C (375°F/Gas Mark 5)

1. Wash the leeks in cold water, drain thoroughly. Cut the prawns into small pieces and place in a 1 litre Bowl. Add the leeks, Ricotta and seasoning and mix thoroughly.
2. Place the mixture in a large piping bag fitted with a plain 2cm (³/₄in) nozzle and pipe the filling into the cannelloni tubes. (Alternatively, spoon the mixture in.) Place the filled tubes in a large ovenproof dish.
3. Heat the oil and gently fry the onion and garlic for 5 minutes until soft. Add the tomatoes, wine and sugar and bring to the boil.
4. Mix the cornflour and water and add with the basil to the saucepan. Cook until slightly thickened. Adjust seasoning and pour over the cannelloni, making sure all the pasta is covered. Sprinkle with the cheese and bake for 20 minutes until brown and bubbling.

Serves 4

Easy-cook cannelloni requires no pre-cooking and so is simpler to handle and fill. However, the pasta must be completely covered with sauce. So if you are cooking more than one layer in the dish, the bottom layer must be covered in sauce before the second layer is placed on top.

CHICKEN AND SAFFRON RICE RING

Preparation time : 25 minutes
Cooling time : 2 hours
Calories per serving : 394

225g (8oz) long grain rice
few strands saffron
1 stick lemon grass, crushed
100g (4oz) fine asparagus
1 red pepper, diced
75g (3oz) frozen peas
75g (3oz) frozen sweetcorn
225g (8oz) cooked chicken meat
3tbsp chopped fresh parsley
4tbsp walnut oil
2tbsp white wine vinegar
1tsp coarse grain mustard
2tsp caster sugar
salt and freshly ground black pepper

1. Cook the rice, saffron and lemon grass using the Multi-Server (page 70).
2. Cut the asparagus into 1cm (¹/₂in) pieces and place in a saucepan with the red pepper, peas and sweetcorn. Add boiling water and return to the boil. Refresh in plenty of cold water, using the Double Colander, and drain thoroughly.
3. Cut the chicken into 1cm (¹/₂in) cubes. Remove the lemon grass from the rice and place the latter in a 3 litre Bowl with the vegetables, chicken and parsley. Place the remaining ingredients in a Quick Shake and blend well. Pour over the rice mixture and mix thoroughly.
4. Transfer the rice mixture to a 1.5 litre Jel Ring, gently pressing down into the mould. Seal and leave for 2 hours before turning out on to a Serve-it-All plate.

Serves 4

This is ideal for picnics. Simply transport in the Jel Ring and turn out when needed for an extra special touch.

Ricotta should be eaten on the day you buy it. It's ideal for making cheesecake as it is smooth and almost salt-free.

Double Colander
An example of Tupperware attention to detail: the shallow colander fits neatly on top of the larger, allowing salads to be shaken dry. It also provides an ideal surface to rinse more delicate foods.

TOP *Chicken and Saffron Rice Ring* BOTTOM *Cannelloni with Ricotta*

TOP *Spinach & Pine Nut Lasagne* CENTRE *Penne Carnevale* BOTTOM *Pasta Shells in Rosemary Sauce*

50

SPINACH AND PINE NUT LASAGNE

Preparation time : 25 minutes
Cooking time : 30 minutes
Calories per serving : 527-790

3 quantities white sauce (page 126)
9 sheets easy-cook lasagne
900g (2lb) spinach (frozen or fresh), cooked and squeezed dry
50g (2oz) pine nuts
100g (4oz) Mozzarella cheese, grated
100g (4oz) Red Leicester cheese, grated
75g (3oz) Parmesan cheese, grated

Preheat oven to 190°C (375°F/Gas Mark 5)

1. Make the white sauce with the Quick Shake, and cook until thickened.
2. Pour one third of the sauce into the bottom of a large lasagne dish approximately 30cm x 23cm (12in x 9in), and place 3 pasta sheets on top. Spread half of the spinach evenly over the pasta and sprinkle half of the pine nuts on top.
3. Add a layer of Mozzarella cheese, place 3 more pasta sheets on top and pour over another third of the sauce. Distribute the remainder of the spinach over the sauce and add the Red Leicester cheese.
4. Place the remaining 3 pasta sheets on top and pour over the remaining sauce. Sprinkle the Parmesan cheese and remaining pine nuts over the top and bake for 30 minutes until brown.

Serves 4-6

PASTA SHELLS IN ROSEMARY SAUCE

Preparation time : 5 minutes
Cooking time : 15 minutes
Calories per serving : 1004

4 cloves garlic, peeled and crushed
25g (1oz) fresh rosemary
75g (3oz) Macadamia nuts
100g (4oz) Parmesan cheese, grated
7 sun-dried tomatoes
150ml (¼ pint) olive oil
350g (12oz) dried pasta shells

1. Blend all the ingredients except the pasta shells in a liquidiser or food processor for 3 minutes, until a thick sauce is formed. Transfer and store in a Black and Clear Jam Dish.
2. Cook the pasta shells in the Multi-Server (page 70). Serve immediately with the rosemary sauce.

Serves 4

This sauce keeps very well and the flavour improves after 24 hours. To prevent the sauce from cooling the pasta too much, you can warm the sauce before serving it.

PENNE CARNEVALE

Preparation time : 15 minutes
Cooking time : 15 minutes
Calories per serving : 421

225g (8oz) penne pasta
1tbsp vegetable oil
1 medium onion, chopped
2 cloves garlic, finely chopped
1 red pepper, diced
1tsp chilli powder (or to taste)
1tsp paprika
2tbsp tomato purée
150ml (¼ pint) white wine
1 quantity white sauce mixture (page 126)
3 large tomatoes, peeled, seeded and chopped
100g (4oz) ham, cut into strips
50g (2oz) frozen peas
2tbsp chopped fresh parsley
salt and freshly ground black pepper

1. Cook the penne in the Multi-Server (page 70).
2. Heat the oil and gently fry the onion, garlic and pepper for 5 minutes. Add the chilli powder, paprika and tomato purée, and cook for 1 minute. Pour in the wine and boil rapidly for 2 minutes.
3. Add the white sauce mixture and cook, stirring until the sauce has thickened. Add the chopped tomatoes, ham, peas and parsley and cook for 2 more minutes; adjust seasoning. Add the pasta to the sauce and stir thoroughly.

Serves 4

Easy-cook lasagne does not require pre-cooking and is simpler and easier to handle.

Try substituting turkey mince for the beef in your usual Bolognese sauce recipe. The result will be lighter tasting and much lower in fat, and therefore in calories. It will also save time as the turkey will cook more quickly than beef.

JAMBALAYA

Preparation time : 15 minutes
Cooking time : 35 minutes
Calories per serving : 524

225g (8oz) long grain rice
one 397g (14oz) can tomatoes
100g (4oz) chorizo sausage, sliced
1tbsp vegetable oil
1 medium onion, finely chopped
2 cloves garlic, finely chopped
1 red pepper, diced
1 green pepper, diced
$^{1}/_{2}$tsp chilli powder
1tsp cayenne pepper
1tbsp tomato purée
1tsp chopped fresh thyme (or $^{1}/_{2}$ tsp dried)
175g (6oz) ham, diced
225g (8oz) peeled prawns
2tbsp chopped fresh parsley for garnish

1. Cook the rice in the Multi-Server (page 70).
2. Blend the canned tomatoes to a pulp in a liquidiser or food processor.
3. In a saucepan, fry the chorizo sausage without oil, until brown; transfer to a Tropical Serving Cup and pour away the fat from the pan. Heat the oil and gently fry the onion, garlic, and red and green peppers for 5 minutes. Add the chilli and cayenne pepper and cook for a further minute.
4. Add the tomato purée, thyme and liquidised tomatoes, and bring to the boil. Stir in the ham, prawns, sausage and rice; return to the boil and then simmer for 5 minutes. Sprinkle with parsley before serving.

Serves 4

Jambalaya is one of the best known Creole Cajun dishes from America's Deep South. The name comes from the Spanish *jamón*, ham. There are many versions, but most include ham, prawns and rice.

Pepperoni sausage is a good alternative if chorizo is unobtainable.

SEAFOOD TAGLIATELLE

Preparation time : 20 minutes
Cooking time : 15 minutes
Calories per serving : 661

350g (12oz) tagliatelle verdi
225g (8oz) Queen scallops
225g (8oz) monkfish
2tbsp olive oil
2 shallots, finely chopped
2 cloves garlic, finely chopped
100g (4oz) button mushrooms, halved
150ml ($^{1}/_{4}$ pint) white wine
450g (1lb) tomatoes, peeled, quartered
and seeded
225g (8oz) cooked mussels
225g (8oz) peeled prawns
1tbsp cornflour
2tbsp cold water
salt and freshly ground black pepper
2tbsp chopped fresh dill (or 2tsp dried)

1. Cook the tagliatelle in the Multi-Server (page 70).
2. Separate the coral from the scallops and cut the white meat in half horizontally. Cut the monkfish into large chunks.
3. In a large frying pan, heat the oil and fry the shallots, garlic and mushrooms for 2 minutes. Add the scallops (coral and white meat) and monkfish and stir-fry for a further 3 minutes over a high heat.
4. Add the wine and tomatoes to the pan, bring to the boil and cook rapidly for 3 minutes. Add the mussels and prawns and heat through. Thicken the sauce slightly with the cornflour and water mixture. Adjust seasoning and add the dill.
5. To serve, divide the tagliatelle between 4 plates and pour the seafood sauce in the centre of each.

Serves 4

Wash and dry fresh herbs well before you chop them. That way they won't stick to the knife or chopping board.

We are fast becoming used to green pasta, flavoured with spinach, and red pasta, flavoured with tomato. But in Italy flavourings include artichoke and savoury chocolate - and black pasta which has been coloured and flavoured with squids' ink.

TOP *Jambalaya* BOTTOM *Seafood Tagliatelle*

5
Vegetables & Salads

Celery was used by the Ancient Greeks and Romans for medicinal purposes. The first recorded use of it as a food was in 16th-century France.

Chop n Grate
Save time by grating, slicing, shredding or chopping with one product. Two inserts and a chopping board give you maximum flexibility when working, and will fit over most sizes of Tupperware bowls.

SMOKED CHICKEN SALAD

Preparation time : 25 minutes
Calories per serving : 380

•

450g (1lb) smoked chicken breast fillet
2 peaches
1 head frisée (curly endive)
1 head radicchio
100g (4oz) lamb's lettuce
3tbsp olive oil
2tbsp lime juice cordial
1tsp Dijon mustard
2tsp chopped fresh chives
salt and freshly ground black pepper
50g (2oz) cashew nuts, roasted
chives for garnish (uncut)

1. Slice the smoked chicken thinly. Peel and stone the peaches and cut into thin slices. Using the Double Colander, wash and thoroughly dry the salad leaves.
2. Place the olive oil, lime juice cordial, mustard, chives, salt and pepper in the Quick Shake and mix thoroughly.
3. Arrange the chicken, peaches, and salad leaves attractively on 4 plates. Sprinkle each with cashew nuts and pour a little dressing over. Place a few strips of chives over the salad to garnish.

Serves 4

Mangoes or other soft fruits make good alternatives if fresh peaches are not available.

Any leftover salad leaves can be stored in the Tropical Crisper.

PATATE ROMA

Preparation time : 15 minutes
Cooking time : 40 minutes
Calories per serving : 220

•

900g (2lb) potatoes
2tbsp chopped fresh rosemary
2 cloves garlic, finely chopped
salt and freshly ground black pepper
150ml (¼ pint) vegetable stock (page 126)
25g (1oz) butter

Preheat oven to 190°C (375°F/Gas Mark 5)

1. Peel the potatoes and cut into thin slices using the Chop n Grate.
2. Place the slices in a 3 litre Bowl and sprinkle over them the rosemary, garlic, salt and pepper. Mix well.
3. Layer the potato mixture in a 900ml (1½ pint) ovenproof dish, bring the stock to the boil and pour over the potatoes.
4. Dot with small pieces of butter; bake for 40 minutes until crisp and brown on top.

Serves 4

SPROUTING BEAN SALAD

Preparation time : 15 minutes
Marinating time : 1 hour
Calories per serving : 80

•

2 oranges, peeled and segmented
100g (4oz) button mushrooms, thinly sliced
150g (5oz) sprouting bean mixture or beansprouts
2tbsp walnut oil
2tbsp freshly squeezed orange juice
1tsp coarse grain mustard
salt and freshly ground black pepper

1. Mix the oranges, mushrooms and beansprouts in a 1.5 litre Bowl.
2. Place the remaining ingredients in the Quick Shake and blend thoroughly.
3. Add the dressing to the orange mixture and combine well. Seal and leave for 1 hour before serving.

Serves 4

It is possible to sprout beans at home using the Multi-Server. Fill a 100ml Measuring Cup with the bean of your choice and pour into the colander of the Multi-Server. Wash in plenty of cold water and then cover and leave to soak in clean, cold water overnight. Wash the beans in more cold water, drain and replace in the Multi-Server twice a day for several days, until they start to sprout. When they are about 2.5cm (1in) long, use for stir-fries or in salads.

TOP *Patate Roma* CENTRE *Sprouting Bean Salad* BOTTOM *Smoked Chicken Salad*

55

TOP *Japanese Bean Salad* CENTRE *Scrumpy Red Cabbage* BOTTOM *Pepper Salad*

JAPANESE BEAN SALAD

Preparation time : 15 minutes
Cooking time : 3 minutes
Marinating time : 1 hour
Calories per serving : 65

•

225g (8oz) Kenyan green beans
1tsp salt
100g (4oz) carrot
100g (4oz) mooli
2tbsp tahini (sesame paste)
1tsp sherry
2tbsp light soy sauce
2tsp honey
1tbsp white wine vinegar
1tbsp lemon juice
1tbsp sesame seeds, toasted

1. Trim the beans and cut in half diagonally. Place the beans in a pan of boiling water with the salt and cook for 3 minutes. Refresh in cold water, drain thoroughly and place in a 2 litre Bowl.
2. Peel and cut the carrot and mooli into thin sticks about 5cm (2in) long. Blanch in boiling water and refresh in cold water. Drain and mix with the beans.
3. Mix the tahini, sherry, soy sauce, honey, vinegar and lemon juice in the Quick Shake and add to the bean mixture. Stir thoroughly and leave for 1 hour.
4. Sprinkle with sesame seeds.

Serves 6

PEPPER SALAD

Preparation time : 30 minutes
Marinating time : 4 hours
Calories per serving : 146

•

2 red peppers
1 green pepper
1 orange or yellow pepper
15g (1/2oz) capers
16 black olives
one 50g (1.76oz) can anchovy fillets, drained
3tbsp olive oil
1tbsp chopped fresh parsley
1 clove garlic, finely chopped
1tsp coarse grain mustard
2tbsp freshly squeezed lime juice
salt

1. Char the whole peppers under a preheated hot grill, turning frequently to brown evenly. Allow to cool for 5 minutes.
2. Peel the peppers, remove the stalks and seeds and cut into 1cm (1/2 in) wide strips. Place in a 1 litre Bowl with the capers, olives and anchovies.
3. Mix the remaining ingredients in the Quick Shake and pour over the pepper mixture. Mix thoroughly. Seal and leave to marinate for 4 hours, or overnight, before serving.

Serves 4

SCRUMPY RED CABBAGE

Preparation time : 15 minutes
Cooking time : 20 minutes
Calories per serving : 165

•

350g (12oz) Golden Delicious apples
350g (12oz) red cabbage
1tbsp vegetable oil
2tbsp grated fresh ginger
100g (4oz) carrot, grated
225g (8oz) pineapple, cut into chunks
75g (3oz) sultanas
150ml (1/4 pint) sweet cider
salt and freshly ground black pepper

1. Core the apples, but do not peel. Chop into large chunks. Quarter the cabbage, remove the hard centre core and slice into thin strips using the Chop n Grate.
2. Heat the oil and fry the ginger for 1 minute over a medium heat. Add the cabbage and cook for 2 minutes. Add the apples, carrot, pineapple and sultanas and fry for a further 2 minutes, stirring.
3. Add the cider and bring to the boil. Reduce heat and simmer, covered, for 15 minutes. Adjust seasoning before serving.

Serves 4

This cooking time leaves the cabbage fairly crisp. If you prefer well-cooked red cabbage, simmer for a further 15 minutes, adding a little water as necessary to prevent sticking.

Green beans are really fresh if they 'snap' when bent.

Peppers are remarkably high in vitamin C and very low in calories (15 per medium pepper).

SUMMER CAULIFLOWER

Preparation time : 15 minutes
Cooking time : 18 minutes
Calories per serving : 75

•

1 medium cauliflower
25g (1oz) butter
½ red pepper, thinly sliced
½ green pepper, thinly sliced
3tbsp cold water
salt and freshly ground black pepper
2 large tomatoes, skinned, seeded and chopped
2tbsp chopped fresh chives

1. Trim the cauliflower and cut into florets. Place in the colander of the Multi-Server, pour boiling water over till just covered. Seal and leave 10 minutes.
2. Heat the butter and gently fry the peppers for 3 minutes. Drain the cauliflower, add to the saucepan with the cold water and cook for a further 3 minutes.
3. Adjust seasoning and add the chopped tomatoes and chives. Heat through and serve.

Serves 4

PARSNIP SOUFFLÉ

Preparation time : 40 minutes
Cooking time : 30 minutes
Calories per serving : 205

•

450g (1lb) parsnips, peeled and roughly chopped
150ml (¼ pint) milk
15g (½oz) plain flour
25g (1oz) butter
3tbsp chopped fresh parsley (or 1tbsp dried)
3 eggs
salt and freshly ground black pepper

Preheat oven to 200°C (400°F/Gas Mark 6)

1. Cover the parsnips with cold water and bring to the boil. Cover and simmer for 15 minutes until soft.
2. Blend the milk and flour in the Quick Shake. Cook in a small saucepan with the butter, stirring until the butter has melted and the sauce has thickened. Add the parsley and transfer to a Multi Mixing Bowl.
3. Drain the parsnips and mash to a pulp, add to the sauce and mix thoroughly: leave to cool for 15 minutes. Separate the eggs with the Cook's Maid Egg Separator.
4. Beat the yolks into the parsnip mixture and season to taste. Whisk the egg whites until stiff but not dry, and carefully fold into the parsnips. Transfer to a 900ml (1½ pint) soufflé dish and bake for 30 minutes in the centre of the oven, until well-risen and golden brown. Don't open oven door whilst cooking. Serve immediately.

Serves 4-6

LEEKS IN HERB VINAIGRETTE

Preparation time : 5 minutes
Cooking time : 13 minutes
Calories per serving : 87

•

450g (1lb) baby leeks
1tsp salt
2tbsp hazelnut oil
1tbsp red wine vinegar
1tsp coarse grain mustard
1tsp caster sugar
1tbsp chopped fresh parsley
1tbsp chopped fresh tarragon (or 1tsp dried)
salt and freshly ground black pepper

1. Trim and wash the leeks and place in a saucepan with the salt. Pour in boiling water to cover the leeks, return to the boil and cook for 3 minutes until just tender.
2. Put the remaining ingredients into the Quick Shake and mix thoroughly.
3. Drain the leeks well in the Double Colander and place in a warmed serving dish. Pour the dressing over and leave for 10 minutes before serving warm.

Serves 4

This is equally good served chilled: just leave the leeks in the dressing until cold before serving. If baby leeks are not available, then normal-sized leeks can be used.

For a tasty change, try putting French dressing instead of a knob of butter on hot, freshly cooked vegetables.

Tropical Crisper
The Tropical Crisper is a more compact version of the Space Saver Crisper and has the same useful freshness grid to keep salads and vegetables really crisp.

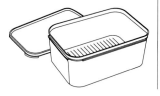

TOP *Summer Cauliflower* CENTRE *Parsnip Soufflé* BOTTOM *Leeks in Herb Vinaigrette*

TOP *Double Vegetable Purée* CENTRE *Fennel au Gratin* BOTTOM *Celery Stir-Fry*

FENNEL AU GRATIN

Preparation time : 5 minutes
Cooking time : 20 minutes
Calories per serving : 183

•

2 fennel, about 175g (6oz) each
1 quantity white sauce (page 126)
50g (2oz) Cheddar cheese, grated
salt and freshly ground black pepper
25g (1oz) fresh breadcrumbs

1. Cut the fennel into quarters vertically. Place in the colander of the Multi-Server and add enough boiling water to just cover. Cover and leave for 15 minutes. Drain well.
2. Make the white sauce, and when boiling, add half the grated cheese. Remove from heat and stir until the cheese is melted. Season to taste. Mix the rest of the cheese and breadcrumbs together.
3. Transfer the fennel into a shallow ovenproof dish, pour the cheese sauce over and sprinkle with the cheese and crumb mixture. Cook under a preheated hot grill until brown and crisp.

Serves 4

This dish may be made up earlier in the day and then heated through in the oven. Simply bake in a preheated oven at 190°C (375°F/Gas Mark 5) for 20 minutes.

CELERY STIR-FRY

Preparation time : 10 minutes
Cooking time : 10 minutes
Calories per serving : 92

•

1 head of celery
1tbsp vegetable oil
50g (2oz) walnut halves
1 clove garlic, finely chopped
3tbsp cold water
3tbsp chopped fresh coriander
salt

1. Wash and cut the celery diagonally into 1cm (½in) slices.
2. Heat the oil and fry the walnuts for 2 minutes over a medium heat. Add the garlic and fry for 15 seconds. Turn the heat

up to high and add the celery. Stir-fry for 2 minutes.
3. Add the water and continue cooking for 3 minutes. Remove from heat, and stir in the coriander. Add salt to taste.
4. Transfer to the Servalier to serve.

Serves 4

DOUBLE VEGETABLE PURÉE

Preparation time : 15 minutes
Cooking time : 20 minutes
Calories per serving : 192

•

900g (2lb) celeriac
100g (4oz) potato
25g (1oz) butter
1tbsp vegetable oil
1 small onion, chopped
2 cloves garlic, crushed
900g (2lb) brussel sprouts, trimmed
6tbsp cold water
salt and freshly ground black pepper
4tbsp chopped fresh coriander
15g (½oz) flaked almonds, toasted

1. Peel the celeriac and potato and cut into 2.5cm (1in) cubes. Heat the butter in a saucepan, add the celeriac and potato and cook covered for 20 minutes over a low heat. Shake the pan occasionally to prevent burning, but do not lift the lid.
2. Heat the oil in a large saucepan and fry the onion and garlic for 1 minute over a high heat. Add the sprouts and water, reduce heat to low, cover and cook for 10 minutes. Shake the pan occasionally to prevent burning, but do not lift the lid.
3. Transfer the sprout mixture to a liquidiser or food processor, season and blend to a purée. Place in one half of the Servalier to keep warm.
4. Rinse out the liquidiser or food processor and purée the celeriac and potato mixture, adding the coriander and seasoning for the last 30 seconds. Serve in the Servalier with the brussel sprout purée.
5. Sprinkle toasted almonds over the sprouts just before serving to add crunch.

Serves 4

When storing brussel sprouts in Tupperware containers, put in a small piece of peeled carrot with them. It prevents smells.

Servalier
Can be used to serve vegetables, casseroles and a wide variety of meat or fish dishes. The inner drainer keeps rice and pasta al dente by draining off excess moisture.

6
Desserts

When whipping cream in the 1 litre Mix n Stor, add another 50 per cent of milk and beat. It makes it lighter and it goes further.

Domed Server
A generous size to protect and serve the most lavish of gâteaux or special desserts. The dome fits snugly on the base keeping the cake fresher for longer too. You can use the pedestal from the Serve-it-All as a stand.

DUTCH APPLE PANCAKE

Preparation time : 10 minutes
Cooking time : 45 minutes
Calories per serving : 210-315

•

1 medium lemon
900g (2lb) Golden Delicious apples, peeled, cored and coarsely chopped
4tbsp cold water
100g (4oz) sultanas
4tbsp orange marmalade
1tsp ground cinnamon
1 quantity pancake batter (page 124)
3tbsp icing sugar

1. Use a Cook's Maid to remove the zest and juice of the lemon. Place in a saucepan with the apples, cold water, sultanas and marmalade, and cook over a low heat for 15 minutes, until thick but not mushy. Add the cinnamon and allow to cool.
2. Using the Quick Shake, make eight thin 20cm (8in) pancakes.
3. Assemble the cake on the Domed Server by layering evenly the pancakes with the apple mixture, starting and ending with a pancake.
4. Dust the top with icing sugar and, using heated metal skewers, mark the top with a lattice pattern. Store in the Domed Server until needed, to prevent the top pancake from drying out.
5. Serve with a jug of pouring cream.

Serves 4-6

The pancakes and apple mixture may be made in advance and kept separately frozen in Freeze n Stor containers and assembled when required.

FROZEN AMARETTO MOUSSE

Preparation time : 25 minutes
Freezing time : 6 hours
Calories per serving : 228-304

•

3 eggs
300ml (½ pint) whipping cream

75g (3oz) caster sugar
4tbsp Amaretto liqueur
75g (3oz) Amaretti biscuits, crushed

1. Separate the eggs with the Cook's Maid. Place the yolks in a 2 litre Mix n Stor and the whites in a 1.5 litre Bowl. Measure the cream into a 1 litre Mix n Stor and set to one side.
2. Add the sugar to the yolks and set the Mix n Stor inside a Multi-Server half filled with boiling water. Whisk with an electric whisk until pale and frothy. Add the Amaretto and continue to whisk for approximately 10 minutes, until the mixture leaves a trail which lasts for a count of 5.
3. Whisk the egg whites until stiff but not dry and then whisk the cream, using the same set of beaters.
4. With the Paddle Scraper, carefully fold the cream into the yolk mixture, followed by the crushed Amaretti and finally the egg white. Transfer to a Jel n Serve, seal and freeze for 6 hours, or overnight.
5. To turn out, dip the Jel n Serve quickly into a bowl of boiling water, remove the seal and turn out on to the plate. Serve immediately.

Serves 6-8

Individual servings may be made by freezing the mixture in Tropical Serving Cups or Mini Freezer Containers.

APRICOT CLAFOUTIS

Preparation time : 10 minutes
Cooking time : 40 minutes
Calories per serving : 180-270

•

15g (½oz) butter, melted
450g (1lb) fresh apricots, halved and stoned
2 eggs
50g (2oz) caster sugar
½tsp almond essence
50g (2oz) self-raising flour
25g (1oz) ground almonds
175ml (6fl oz) milk
15g (½oz) flaked almonds
2tbsp icing sugar

TOP *Dutch Apple Pancake* CENTRE *Apricot Clafoutis* BOTTOM *Frozen Amaretto Mousse*

TOP *Dried Fruit Strudel* BOTTOM *Hazelnut & Raspberry Timbale*

Preheat oven to 180°C (350°F/Gas Mark 4)

1. Grease a 1.2 litre (2 pint) shallow ovenproof dish with the melted butter and set to one side. Place the apricots in the prepared dish with the cut face down.
2. Using an electric (or hand) whisk, beat the eggs, sugar and almond essence for 3 minutes in a 2 litre Mix n Stor, until pale and fairly stiff. Whisk in the flour and ground almonds and then the milk, to make a thick batter.
3. Pour over the apricots and sprinkle flaked almonds on top. Bake for 40 minutes in the centre of the oven, until golden brown. Dust with icing sugar and serve with Greek yogurt.

Serves 4-6

Clafoutis is quite a solid batter pudding – do not expect a light sponge! The apricot skins may be removed by blanching in boiling water.

DRIED FRUIT STRUDEL

Preparation time : 15 minutes
Cooking time : 30 minutes
Calories per serving : 206-309

•

225g (8oz) Ricotta cheese
1 egg
50g (2oz) dried apricots, chopped
50g (2oz) dates, chopped
50g (2oz) glacé cherries, quartered
50g (2oz) roasted hazelnuts, chopped
1tsp mixed spice
zest of 1 lemon
4 sheets filo pastry, about 38cm x 19cm (15in x 7¹/₂in)
3tbsp walnut oil
2tbsp icing sugar

Preheat oven to 200°C (400°F/Gas Mark 6)

1. In a Multi Mixing Bowl beat the cheese and egg together, add the dried fruit, hazelnuts, spice and lemon zest. Mix well.
2. Place one sheet of filo pastry on the Pastry Sheet and brush a little walnut oil on top; place another sheet of pastry on top and brush with oil. Repeat with the

remaining pastry sheets.
3. Pile the fruit filling on to one third of the pastry lengthways, leaving 2.5cm (1in) clear at each of the short ends. With the help of the Pastry Sheet, roll up the pastry, finishing with the join under the roll. Close the open ends and tuck underneath.
4. Transfer on to a greased baking tray. Brush the top with a little walnut oil, and bake for 25-30 minutes in the centre of the oven, until brown.
5. Dust with icing sugar and serve hot or cold with pouring cream.

Serves 4-6

HAZELNUT AND RASPBERRY TIMBALE

Preparation time : 15 minutes
Chilling time : 3 hours
Calories per serving : 290

•

2tsp hazelnut oil
2tsp gelatine
2tbsp cold water
150ml (¹/₄ pint) whipping cream
300ml (¹/₂ pint) Greek yogurt
4tbsp clear honey
175g (6oz) ground roasted hazelnuts
¹/₂ tsp mixed spice
225g (8oz) fresh raspberries
50g (2oz) caster sugar

1. Lightly coat 6 Egg Cup covers with hazelnut oil and place upside down on kitchen paper to drain off excess oil.
2. Sprinkle the gelatine on to the water and dissolve in the Multi-Server (page 70).
3. Shake the cream in the Quick Shake until fairly stiff. Set to one side. Mix the yogurt, honey, hazelnuts and spice in a 1 litre Mix n Stor, stir in the gelatine and finally fold in the whipped cream. Pour the mixture into the Egg Cup covers. Place the filled covers in a Square 2 container. (This makes them easy to handle and prevents other flavours from being absorbed.) Seal and refrigerate for 3 hours.
4. Reserve 18 raspberries and place the remainder in a liquidiser or food processor with the sugar and blend for 1 minute. Strain to remove the pips.

Use the Quick Shake to whip cream without electricity. Chill the cream, place in the Quick Shake, and shake vigorously for 3-4 minutes until you have the desired thickness.

Use Egg Cup covers for serving children's portions of blancmange, jelly or homemade yogurt.

5. To serve, tilt each cover downward and carefully slide a flexible knife a little way down the side of the cover and press gently against the hazelnut cream to loosen. (You may need to do this several times.) Turn each one out on to a serving plate, pour a pool of raspberry sauce around each and top with 3 raspberries.

Serves 6

For a really professional finish, carefully drop spots of unwhipped cream on to the raspberry sauce around each timbale and draw through with a cocktail stick to make a marbled pattern.

BOOZY FONDUE

Preparation time : 15 minutes
Cooking time : 10 minutes
Calories per serving : 274

•

2 medium red apples
175g (6oz) strawberries
2 kiwi fruits
1 baby pineapple
1tbsp cornflour
150ml ($^1/_4$ pint) sweet dessert wine
150ml ($^1/_4$ pint) single cream
zest of 1 medium orange
2 egg yolks
100g (4oz) any delicate sweet biscuits
few small fresh mint leaves for decoration

1. Quarter the apples, remove the core and cut into thick slices. Wash the strawberries but keep the stalks on. Peel the kiwi fruit and cut lengthways into wedges. Cut the pineapple into 2cm ($^3/_4$in) slices, with the skin on, and then quarter each slice. Place the fruit in a Tropical Crisper, seal and refrigerate until needed.
2. Mix the cornflour with the wine and pour into a small saucepan. Add the cream and orange zest and bring to the boil, stirring constantly. When thickened, whisk into the egg yolks with a hand whisk.
3. Almost fill the smaller of the two spaces in the Serve-it-All stand with boiling water. Secure the base dish on to the stand to retain the water and turn over, so that the empty space of the stand is uppermost.

4. Arrange the fruit and biscuits on the dish around the stand. Pour the wine mixture into the stand, scatter the mint leaves over the top and serve immediately.

Serves 4

MANGO SORBET WITH STRAWBERRY SAUCE

Preparation time : 15 minutes
Freezing time : 6 hours
Calories per serving : 172-229

•

two 439g (15oz) cans of mango
1 lime, juice and zest
300ml ($^1/_2$ pint) sweet white wine
2 egg whites
100g (4oz) caster sugar
225g (8oz) ripe strawberries
75g (3oz) caster sugar

1. Strain the mango to remove the juice and then purée in a liquidiser or food processor. Add the lime juice, zest and wine. Blend for a further 30 seconds.
2. Whisk the egg whites until frothy, add the 100g (4oz) of sugar and continue to whisk until stiff but not dry.
3. Carefully fold the egg whites into the mango mixture and transfer to a 1.3 litre Freeze n Stor. Seal and freeze for 6 hours.
4. Blend the strawberries and remaining sugar in a liquidiser or food processor for 1 minute. Strain the purée through a sieve and store in a Black and Clear Jug. To serve, place spoonfuls of the sorbet on each plate and top with strawberry sauce.

Serves 6-8

WINTER PUDDING

Preparation time : 45 minutes
Chilling time : overnight
Calories per serving : 276-368

•

1 litre (1 $^3/_4$ pints) strong black tea
rind of 1 lemon
1 cinnamon stick
10 cloves
75g (3oz) dried figs
75g (3oz) dried apricots
75g (3oz) prunes

Store eggs with the pointed end down, as this keeps the air pocket up at the round end and slows down any deterioration. The less fresh the egg, the less flavour.

Serve-it-All
For dips, crudités, hors d'oeuvres, cheeses or fruits. This is another useful and versatile item.

TOP *Boozy Fondue* CENTRE *Winter Pudding* BOTTOM *Mango Sorbet with Strawberry Sauce*

TOP *Fruit Trifle Ring* CENTRE *Ginger & Plum Upside-Down Pudding (page 70)* BOTTOM *Moccha Pots*

25g (1oz) dried apple rings
400g (14oz) fruit loaf, cut into 1cm (¹/₂ in) slices
100g (4oz) walnuts, chopped
4tbsp rum

1. Simmer the tea with the lemon rind, cinnamon and cloves for 10 minutes. Strain into a clean saucepan, add the dried fruit and return to the boil. Reduce heat, partially cover and simmer for 20 minutes.
2. Remove the crusts and use all but 3 slices of fruit loaf to line the sides and base of the Jel n Serve, overlapping each slice slightly.
3. Stir the walnuts and rum into the fruit mixture and spoon into the mould, pressing it in firmly. Cover with the reserved slices and seal. Refrigerate overnight.
4. Remove seal and invert on to the plate. Gently loosen the centre seal and lift off the mould. Serve with Greek yogurt.

Serves 6-8

Try making this pudding with different combinations of dried fruit and nuts.

MOCCHA POTS

Preparation time : 15 minutes
Chilling time : 2 hours
Calories per pot : 364
•
200g (7oz) plain chocolate
4tbsp strong black coffee
one 439g (15oz) can cherries, drained
4tbsp kirsch
300ml (¹/₂ pint) fromage frais
15g (¹/₂ oz) plain chocolate curls★
15g (¹/₂ oz) white chocolate curls★
(★see page 124)

1. Put the chocolate and coffee in a Tropical Salad Bowl and place in the Multi-Server to melt the chocolate (page 70).
2. Divide the cherries between 4 Tropical Serving Cups.
3. Add the kirsch to the melted chocolate and stir until smooth. Stir in the fromage frais until well mixed, and pour over the cherries. Smooth the top of the mixture, seal and refrigerate for 2 hours.
4. Decorate with the plain and white chocolate curls just before serving.

Serves 4

FRUIT TRIFLE RING

Preparation time : 2 hours
Chilling time : 4 hours
Calories per serving : 192
•
rind of 1 lemon
one 5cm (2in) cinnamon stick
3 sachets or 9tsp powdered gelatine
300ml (¹/₂ pint) sweet dessert wine
1 passion fruit
2 mini jam rolls, cut into 1cm (¹/₂ in) slices
450g (1lb) fresh raspberries
100g (4oz) caster sugar
2 large peaches
150ml (¹/₄ pint) Greek yogurt

1. Place the lemon rind and cinnamon stick in a saucepan with 150ml (¹/₄ pint) cold water. Bring to the boil, cover and simmer very gently for 5 minutes. Lightly grease the inside and seal of a Jel Ring with vegetable oil and turn upside down on a piece of kitchen towel to drain. Remove the pan from the heat and discard the lemon rind and cinnamon stick. Sprinkle in 3tsp of gelatine, stir until dissolved and add the wine and passion fruit. Mix thoroughly and pour a 1cm (¹/₂ in) layer into the Jel Ring. Refrigerate for 15 minutes to set.
2. Place the jam roll slices on top of the jellied wine and pour another 1cm (¹/₂ in) layer on top. Refrigerate for 15 minutes, then pour the remainder of the wine mix over the jam roll slices and refrigerate for a further 20 minutes.
3. Blend 350g (12oz) raspberries in a liquidiser or food processor with 50g (2oz) sugar for 1 minute. Dissolve 3tsp of gelatine in 4tbsp of hot water. Add to the raspberry purée and make up to 450ml (³/₄ pint) with cold water. Place the remaining raspberries on top of the jellied wine and pour the raspberry purée over. Refrigerate for 30 minutes to set.
4. Dissolve the remaining gelatine in 4tbsp hot water. Blanch the peaches in boiling water, remove the skins and slice. Blend the peaches and the remaining 50g (2oz) sugar in a liquidiser or food processor, until almost liquid but still slightly lumpy. Mix the peach purée with the yogurt and add the dissolved gelatine. Stir to mix

Your mixing bowl won't jump around during whisking if you stand it on a damp cloth.

Jel Ring
Helps create really stunning desserts. The centre seal ensures perfect results every time. Can also be used as a ring mould for rice dishes.

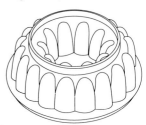

thoroughly and gently add to the Jel Ring. This will cover the whole of the Ring, including the centre. Seal carefully and refrigerate for 4 hours to set.

5. Remove the seal and invert the Jel Ring on to the Serve-it-All plate. Gently loosen the centre seal and lift off the mould. The centre hole may be filled with fresh fruit.

Serves 6

GINGER AND PLUM UPSIDE-DOWN PUDDING

Preparation time : 15 minutes
Cooking time : 1 hour
Calories per serving : 360

•

15g (¹/₂oz) butter, melted
25g (1oz) soft brown sugar
50g (2oz) preserved ginger in syrup, chopped
225g (8oz) red plums, slightly unripe
100g (4oz) soft margarine
100g (4oz) self-raising flour
1tsp baking powder
2tsp ground ginger
100g (4oz) caster sugar
2 eggs
50g (2oz) preserved ginger in syrup, chopped

Preheat oven to 170°C (325°F/Gas Mark 3)

1. Brush the inside of an 18cm (7in) cake tin with the melted butter, line the base with greaseproof paper and brush with butter.

2. Sprinkle the sugar and then the preserved ginger on to the bottom of the tin.

3. Halve and stone the plums. Place them cut face down on the bottom of the tin.

4. Place the margarine, flour, baking powder, ground ginger, sugar and eggs into a 2 litre Mix n Stor, and beat until well blended. Carefully fold in the preserved ginger and pour into the tin. Smooth the top and bake for 1 hour in the centre of the oven.

5. Leave to cool for 5 minutes, then invert on to a serving plate and remove the paper. Serve hot or warm with custard.

Serves 6

DOUBLE CHOCOLATE CROWN

Preparation time : 1 hour 30 minutes
Cooling time : 4 hours
Calories per serving : 281-374

•

100g (4oz) long grain rice
600ml (1 pint) milk
100g (4oz) sugar
2 eggs
1 sachet gelatine
75g (3oz) white chocolate
75g (3oz) plain chocolate
300ml (¹/₂ pint) fromage frais
15g (¹/₂oz) plain chocolate curls (page 124)

1. Cook the rice in the Multi-Server. When cooked, rinse in cold water until the water runs clear, then place in a large saucepan with the milk and sugar. Bring to the boil, partially cover and simmer over a low heat for 45 minutes, stirring occasionally to prevent sticking. Allow to cool for 10 minutes.

2. Separate the eggs with the Cook's Maid Egg Separator and add the yolks to the rice, stirring until well blended. Sprinkle the gelatine over the rice and stir to mix well.

3. Separate the rice into 2 bowls and add white chocolate to one bowl and plain chocolate to the other. Stir until the chocolate has melted and mixed well. Stir half the fromage frais into each bowl and then stand in a basin of cold water to cool for about 5 minutes. Do not let the mixture set.

4. Whisk the egg whites until stiff but not dry, and gently fold one half into each bowl of rice. Transfer the white mixture into a Jel Ring, smooth the top and then carefully spoon in the dark mixture to make 2 layers. Seal and refrigerate for 4 hours to set.

5. To turn out, remove the seal and invert on to a Serve-it-All plate. Loosen the centre seal and carefully lift the Jel Ring out. Decorate with chocolate curls.

Serves 6-8

MULTI-SERVER

To cook rice: *Part-cook rice for 6 minutes before pouring into Multi-Server. Cover and leave for 20 minutes.*

To cook pasta: *Cover completely with boiling water. Add 1tsp oil. Cover and leave for about 15 minutes.*

To melt chocolate: *Pour 900ml (1¹/₂ pints) boiling water into bowl of Multi-Server. Put chocolate in Tropical Salad Bowl and place on colander. Cover and leave for 10-15 minutes.*

To dissolve gelatine: *Pour 900ml (1¹/₂ pints) boiling water into bowl of Multi-Server. Sprinkle gelatine over warm water in a Tropical Serving Cup. Place cup on colander. Cover and leave for 10-15 minutes.*

Double Chocolate Crown

7
Microwave

CHICKEN WITH GRAPEFRUIT

Preparation time : 5 minutes
Marinating time : 1 hour
Cooking time : 30 minutes
Standing time : 5-10 minutes
Calories per serving : 365

•

one 539g (1lb 3oz) can grapefruit segments in natural juice
50g (2oz) demerara sugar
1tbsp white wine vinegar
1-2tbsp prepared chilli and ginger sauce (to taste)
4 boneless chicken breasts, about 125g-175g (4oz-6oz) each, skinned
1 medium leek, sliced
1 red pepper, cut into strips
salt and freshly ground black pepper

Microwave power settings : 100%/Full & 70%

1. Mix together the grapefruit segments and juice, sugar, vinegar and chilli and ginger sauce. Coat the chicken with the marinade in a 1.5 litre or 2 litre TupperWave 200 dish, covered, and leave for at least 1 hour.
2. Add the leek and pepper to the chicken, cover, and cook for 10 minutes on 100%/Full power and a further 20 minutes on 70%, or until the chicken is tender.
3. Leave to stand for 5-10 minutes. Adjust seasoning, and liquidise the sauce before serving.

Serves 4

The sauce will be a very pretty pink from the pepper being liquidised into the grapefruit. For a slightly thicker sauce, remove a few grapefruit segments with a little juice from the can before preparing the marinade.

LAMB FILLET WITH AUBERGINE

Preparation time : 12-15 minutes
Cooking time : 46 minutes
Standing time : 10 minutes
Calories per serving : 286

•

2tbsp vegetable oil

1tsp ground ginger
2tsp ground cumin
1tbsp poppy seeds
1 medium onion, finely sliced
1 small aubergine, halved and sliced
450g (1lb) lamb neck fillet, trimmed and cut into slices
one 397g (14oz) can chopped tomatoes
1tbsp tomato purée
salt and freshly ground black pepper
1 bay leaf

Microwave power settings : 100%/Full & 50%

1. Place the oil, ginger, cumin and poppy seeds in a 1.5 litre TupperWave 200 dish, cover and cook for 1 minute on 100%/Full power. Add the onion and aubergine, stir well, cover and cook for 4-6 minutes on 100%/Full power, until tender. Stir once during cooking.
2. Add the lamb to the vegetables, stir and cook for a further 4 minutes on 100%/Full power, covered. Stir once during cooking.
3. Mix together the tomatoes and the purée and add to the dish with the salt, pepper and bay leaf. Cover and cook for 10 minutes on 100%/Full power.
4. Cook for a further 25 minutes on 50% power, or until tender. Leave to stand for 10 minutes. Adjust seasoning and serve.

Serves 4

To make this casserole go further, add a drained 397g (14oz) can of chick peas during the last 10 minutes on 50% power.

GREEK PEPPER CASSEROLE

Preparation time : 5 minutes
Cooking time : 15 minutes
Calories per serving : 165

•

450g (1lb) mixed coloured peppers, cut into strips
1 medium onion, finely sliced
2 cloves garlic, crushed
3tbsp olive oil
salt and freshly ground black pepper
100g (4oz) Feta cheese, cut into slivers

Microwave power setting : 100%/Full

TOP *Lamb Fillet with Aubergine* CENTRE *Greek Pepper Casserole* BOTTOM *Chicken with Grapefruit*

73

TOP *Peanut & Beansprout Risotto* CENTRE *Dijon Kidneys* BOTTOM *Sweet Potatoes with Coriander*

1. Place the peppers in a 1 litre TupperWave 200 dish with the onion, garlic and oil. Stir well.
2. Cover the dish and cook the peppers for 8-10 minutes, until soft, stirring once during cooking.
3. Remove the cover and season the peppers to taste. Scatter the cheese over the peppers and cook for a further 5-6 minutes, uncovered, until the cheese starts to brown. Serve immediately.

Serves 4

Peppers are like onions – the longer you cook them, the sweeter they become. These peppers really taste of the sun!

SWEET POTATOES WITH CORIANDER

Preparation time : 5 minutes
Cooking time : 12 minutes
Standing time : 2-3 minutes
Calories per serving : 260-350

•

2tbsp vegetable oil
1tbsp coriander seeds
1tsp ground turmeric
1/2 tsp ground chilli
450g (1lb) sweet potatoes, peeled and cut into matchsticks
1 medium onion, finely sliced
150ml (1/4 pint) boiling vegetable stock (page 126)
salt and freshly ground black pepper
150ml (5fl oz) sour cream
1tbsp chopped fresh coriander or parsley for garnish

Microwave power setting : 100%/Full

1. Heat the oil in a 1 litre or 1.5 litre TupperWave 200 dish for 1 minute with the spices. Add the sweet potatoes and onion and stir well. Cover and cook for 6 minutes, stirring once during cooking.
2. Add the vegetable stock and cook for a further 5 minutes. Allow to stand for 2-3 minutes.
3. Adjust seasoning. Stir in the sour cream and serve immediately, garnished with the coriander or parsley.

Serves 3-4

DIJON KIDNEYS

Preparation time : 5-10 minutes
Cooking time : 14 minutes
Standing time : 5 minutes
Calories per serving : 258

•

12 large lambs' kidneys, about 900g (2lb)
1tbsp plain wholemeal flour
2tbsp Dijon mustard
150ml (1/4 pint) red wine
salt and freshly ground black pepper

Microwave power settings : 100%/Full & 70%

1. Core and chop the kidneys. Place them in a 1.5 litre TupperWave 200 dish and stir in the flour. Cook, covered, for 4 minutes, stirring after 2 minutes.
2. Add the mustard and wine, and season to taste. Cover and cook for 10 minutes on 70%, then leave to stand for 5 minutes.
3. Adjust seasoning and serve with plain boiled rice.

Serves 4

The easiest way to prepare kidneys is with a pair of kitchen scissors: snip off each end, then just cut round the core and discard it.

PEANUT AND BEANSPROUT RISOTTO

Preparation time : 10-15 minutes
Cooking time : 10 minutes
Calories per serving : 398

•

225g (8oz) long grain rice, cooked
1 large onion, sliced
1 green pepper, cut into strips
1 small green chilli, finely chopped (optional)
100g (4oz) button mushrooms, sliced
4 eggs, hard-boiled
2tbsp tamari or soy sauce
50g (2oz) peanuts
175g (6oz) beansprouts
2tbsp chopped fresh coriander or parsley

Microwave power setting : 100%/Full

Use your microwave to skin peppers quickly and easily. Cut the pepper into quarters, cook on full power for 1-2 minutes, then peel off the skin.

Red Leicester cheese is ideal for cooking in a microwave. With its strong colour it will add eye-appeal to dishes which would not otherwise brown in a microwave.

1. Put the onion, pepper and chilli (if used) in a 2 litre TupperWave 200 dish. Cover and cook for 3 minutes on 100%/Full power, stirring once.

2. Add the rice and mushrooms, cover and cook for a further 3 minutes, stirring once.

3. Chop three of the hard-boiled eggs and cut the remaining one into quarters for garnishing. Add the chopped eggs, tamari sauce, peanuts and beansprouts and heat, uncovered, for a further 3 minutes, stirring once.

4. Stir in 2tbsp of chopped coriander or parsley, then garnish the risotto with the remaining egg and a few coriander or parsley leaves. Serve immediately.

Serves 4

There is quite a bit of stirring in this recipe, but if you were cooking it in a pan on the hob you would be stirring continuously! Peanut and Beansprout Risotto is a dish that will appeal to meat-eaters and vegetarians alike.

TURKEY, MUSHROOMS AND AVOCADO

Preparation time : 5 minutes
Cooking time : 9 minutes
Chilling time (optional) : 1 hour
Calories per serving : 280-560

•

40g (1¹/₂oz) butter
1tsp ground cumin
225g (8oz) boneless turkey breast, cut into thin strips
25g (1oz) plain wholemeal flour
100g (4oz) button mushrooms, thickly sliced
1 lime, juice and zest, using a Cook's Maid
1 large, ripe but firm avocado, cut into chunks
salt and freshly ground black pepper
paprika for garnish

Microwave power setting : 100%/Full

1. Put the butter and cumin in a 1.5 litre TupperWave 200 dish and heat for 1-2 minutes, until the butter has melted.

2. Toss the turkey in the flour, add to the dish and coat the turkey in the melted butter. Cover and cook for 4-5 minutes, stirring once during cooking.

3. Stir in the mushrooms and the lime zest and cook, uncovered, for 2 minutes.

4. Toss the avocado in the lime juice. Season the turkey to taste and carefully stir in the avocado. Garnish with a little paprika. Serve with a side salad.

Serves 4 as a starter or 2 as a main course

This dish can be eaten cold as a delicious salad; add the avocado shortly before serving to avoid discolouration.

MOULES MARINIÈRES

Preparation time : 10 minutes
Cooking time : 10 minutes
Calories per serving : 269

•

700g (1¹/₂lb) mussels, thoroughly cleaned
1tbsp vegetable oil
1 medium onion, finely chopped
1 stalk celery, finely chopped
1 bay leaf
150ml (¹/₄ pint) dry white wine
salt and freshly ground black pepper
2tbsp single or sour cream
1tbsp chopped fresh parsley

Microwave power setting : 100%/Full

1. Pick over the mussels, discarding any that are open (or remain open when sharply tapped) or have cracked shells. Scrape off any barnacles and remove any beards.

2. Put the oil, onion, celery and bay leaf in a covered 2 litre TupperWave 200 dish and cook for 3-4 minutes on 100%/Full power, stirring once. Add the wine and cook for a further 2 minutes.

3. Stir the mussels into the dish, cover and cook for 3-4 minutes, stirring once or twice, until all the shells have opened. Discard any that don't open.

4. Season to taste and stir the cream and parsley into the dish. Serve immediately with French bread.

Serves 2

All fish cooks well in TupperWave in the microwave. The advantage of the covered dish is that the cooking smells are

The avocado contains 11 vitamins, 14 minerals and a higher protein level than any other fruit. It is low in carbohydrates, has no cholesterol and only 23 calories per 25 grams. Which makes it ideal for almost any diet.

TupperWave 200
The TupperWave 200 range was designed specially to go from freezer to microwave to table. Made of a material that is 100 per cent transparent to microwaves for really efficient cooking at all temperatures, each of the sizes has an individual seal for freezer use.

TOP *Moules Marinières* BOTTOM *Turkey, Mushrooms & Avocado*

TOP *Parsnips with Lemon & Honey* CENTRE *Aubergine & Apple Ratatouille* BOTTOM *Dried Fruit Compote*

contained in the oven and do not get around the whole house.

AUBERGINE AND APPLE RATATOUILLE

Preparation time : 5 minutes
Cooking time : 18 minutes
Standing time : 2-3 minutes
Calories per serving : 76

•

1 medium aubergine, halved and sliced
1 large onion, finely sliced
1 red pepper, cut into strips
450g (1lb) cooking apples, peeled, cored and sliced
one 397g (14oz) can chopped tomatoes
salt and freshly ground black pepper

Microwave power setting : 100%/Full

1. Place the aubergine, onion and pepper in a 1.5 litre TupperWave 200 dish, cover and cook for 3 minutes on 100%/Full power. Add the apples and cook for a further 5 minutes, stirring once.
2. Add the chopped tomatoes and cook, covered, for a further 10 minutes. Adjust seasoning, stand for 2-3 minutes, then serve.

Serves 4

This unusual recipe complements any pork dish well. As it is cooked without oil or butter it is low in calories - but no less delicious for that.

PARSNIPS WITH LEMON AND HONEY

Preparation time : 5 minutes
Cooking time : 8 minutes
Standing time : 2-3 minutes
Calories per serving : 98

•

450g (1lb) parsnips, peeled and cut into matchsticks
1 lemon, juice and zest, using a Cook's Maid
1 bay leaf
2tbsp clear honey
good pinch grated nutmeg

salt and freshly ground black pepper

Microwave power setting : 100%/Full

1. Place the parsnips in a 1 litre TupperWave 200 dish with the remaining ingredients, except the salt and pepper. Stir well and cover.
2. Cook for 6-8 minutes on 100%/Full power, stirring once, then stand for 2-3 minutes. Adjust seasoning and serve immediately.

Serves 4

The lemon and honey give a delicious bitter-sweet flavour to the parsnips.

DRIED FRUIT COMPOTE

Preparation time : 10 minutes
Standing time : 1 hour
Cooking time : 10 minutes
Calories per serving : 212

•

225g (8oz) dried fruits (apricots, apples, peaches etc)
300ml (½ pint) apple juice
2tbsp clear honey
pinch grated nutmeg
25g (1oz) Brazil nuts, chopped

Microwave power setting : 100%/Full

1. Place the dried fruit in a 750ml or 1 litre TupperWave 200 dish with the apple juice. Cover the dish and heat for 5 minutes on 100%/Full power, then leave to stand for 1 hour.
2. Stir the honey into the dish with the nutmeg. Cover and cook for 5 minutes on 100%/Full power, stirring once during cooking.
3. Serve hot or cold, topped with Greek yogurt and sprinkled with the nuts.

Serves 4

Soaking time for beans and pulses can also be considerably shortened using the microwave. Place 225g (8oz) dried beans in a 1.5 or 2 litre TupperWave 200 dish. Cover with plenty of boiling water, then cover the dish. Heat for 10 minutes on

Before using the citrus juicer from the Cook's Maid, place the fruit in the microwave for 20 seconds. You will get far more juice.

Aubergine is the French name for eggplant, so-called because the earliest known varieties bore colourful egg-shaped fruits. In 16th-century Spain they were called 'apples of love'.

100%/Full power, then leave for 1 hour. Drain and use as required. Remember always to boil red kidney beans rapidly for 10 minutes at the start of their cooking.

DATE SLICE

Preparation time : 10 minutes
Cooking time : 6 minutes
Calories per serving : 268

•

225g (8oz) dried stoned dates, chopped
150ml (¹/₄ pint) water
1tsp vanilla essence
150g (5oz) butter or margarine
150g (5oz) rolled oats
150g (5oz) soft brown sugar
150g (5oz) plain wholewheat flour

Microwave power setting : 100%/Full

1. Place the dates with the water in a 750ml TupperWave 200 dish and heat for 5 minutes, uncovered, on 100%/Full power. Add the vanilla essence and beat into a smooth purée.
2. Melt the butter in a 1.5 litre TupperWave 200 dish for 1-2 minutes, add the remaining ingredients and mix well.
3. Line the cover of the 1.5 litre TupperWave 200 dish with baking parchment and press half the oat mixture into the lid to make a biscuit base.
4. Spread the date purée over the base, then top with the remaining oat mixture.
5. Cook for 6 minutes on 100%/Full power. Allow to cool for 30 minutes, then remove the slice from the cover. Leave on a wire rack to cool completely before slicing.

Makes 12

For a slightly sharper taste, try using a layer of apple purée instead of dates - you'll need 450g (1lb) cooking apples, stewed with the very minimum of water and no sugar.

CHOCOLATE BISCUIT CAKE

Preparation time : 10 minutes
Chilling time : 2-3 hours
Calories per square : 300

•

225g (8oz) plain chocolate, broken into pieces
50g (2oz) unsalted butter
1 small orange, juice and zest, using a Cook's Maid
25g (1oz) almonds, chopped
25g (1oz) Brazil nuts, chopped
50g (2oz) raisins
175g (6oz) Nice biscuits, roughly broken

Microwave power setting : 100%/Full

1. Place the chocolate and butter in a 1.5 litre TupperWave 200 dish and heat for 2-3 minutes on 100%/Full power until melted. Stir the chocolate as it does tend to stay in squares, even when soft.
2. Stir in the orange zest and juice and heat the mixture for a few seconds if the orange juice makes the chocolate set again.
3. Add all the remaining ingredients and mix well. Press the mixture firmly into a 1.3 litre Freeze n Stor (so it goes into all the corners). Seal and chill for 2-3 hours until set. Turn out on to a plate and cut into squares. Serve with whipped cream.

Makes 8 squares

Everyone has a recipe for refrigerator cake, but this one is very special - the addition of the orange prevents it from being too rich.

To soak dried fruits for the equivalent of 2-3 hours, place them in a covered TupperWave 200 dish and heat on full power for 5 minutes, then leave to stand for 10 minutes. For the equivalent of an overnight soak, the fruits can be left for one hour.

Soak some clean face flannels in water and place in a TupperWave 200 dish, folded or rolled up. Set microwave on high for 2 minutes. Then use to freshen up with after eating things like spare ribs and barbecue food.

TOP *Date Slice* BOTTOM *Chocolate Biscuit Cake*

8
Savouries & Snacks

You can freshen your breath after eating garlic by sucking a cardamom pod.

Party Server
Prepare party nibbles ahead of time, place in the divided main dish and keep them fresh with the Party Server cover.

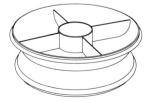

GARLIC TWISTS

Preparation time : 20 minutes
Cooking time : 15 minutes
Calories per twist : 44

•

175g (6oz) plain wholemeal flour
1/2 tsp mustard powder
1/2 tsp salt
75g (3oz) butter
50g (2oz) Gruyère cheese, grated
6 cloves garlic, finely chopped
2tbsp chopped fresh parsley (or 2tsp dried)
1 egg
1 egg yolk

Preheat oven to 190°C (375°F/Gas Mark 5)

1. Using the Sift n Stor, sieve together the flour, mustard and salt into a Multi Mixing Bowl. Rub the butter into the flour until it resembles fine breadcrumbs. Add the cheese, garlic and parsley, and mix thoroughly. Bind with the whole egg, pressing together to form a stiff dough.
2. Dust a Pastry Sheet with flour and roll the dough out into a large rectangle about 3mm (1/8 in) thick. Cut into strips 2cm (3/4 in) wide and divide each strip into 7.5cm (3in) lengths, cutting each piece at an angle. Gather any trimmings together and roll out again.
3. Twist the strips once and place on an ungreased baking tray. Mix the egg yolk with 2tsp cold water and brush lightly over the twists. Bake in the centre of the oven for 12-15 minutes, until brown and crisp. Cool on a wire rack.

Makes about 50 twists

When cooled, store the twists in a Square 2 so they remain crisp.

TUSCANY TRIANGLES

Preparation time : 1 hour
Cooking time : 25 minutes
Calories per triangle : 107

•

2 quantities of shortcrust pastry mix (page 124)
50g (2oz) Parma ham
50g (2oz) Mozzarella cheese, grated
1tbsp chopped fresh marjoram (or 1tsp dried)
1tbsp tomato purée
1 egg yolk, lightly beaten

Preheat oven to 190°C (375°F/Gas Mark 5)

1. Prepare pastry, seal in a Multi Mixing Bowl and chill for 30 minutes.
2. Cut the ham into small pieces and place in a 1 litre Bowl. Add the cheese, marjoram and tomato purée, and mix together.
3. Dust a Pastry Sheet with flour, roll out and trim the pastry to 45cm x 23cm (18in x 9in). Divide the pastry into 7.5cm (3in) squares and place a teaspoonful of filling in the centre of each. Brush the edges with a little water and fold diagonally to form triangles. Press the edges with a fork to seal.
4. Brush the top of each triangle with a little egg yolk and pierce with a fork. Bake for 20-25 minutes in the centre of the oven, until golden brown. Serve hot or cold.

Makes 18

CHEESE GOUGETTES

Preparation time : 25 minutes
Cooking time : 25 minutes
Calories per puff : 61

•

100g (4oz) plain flour
1tsp mustard powder
1tsp paprika
1/4 tsp salt
200ml (7fl oz) cold water
75g (3oz) butter
3 eggs, shaken in a Quick Shake
75g (3oz) Parmesan cheese, grated
225g (8oz) cream cheese
100ml (4fl oz) fromage frais
4tbsp chopped fresh chives
salt and freshly ground black pepper

Preheat oven to 200°C (400°F/Gas Mark 6)

1. Sieve together the flour, mustard, paprika and salt into a Tropical Salad Bowl.
2. Bring the water and butter to the boil in a saucepan. When the butter has melted, remove the pan from the heat and immediately add the flour mixture, stirring vigorously to form a smooth paste. Add the eggs in 4 stages, beating thoroughly between each addition. Add the Parmesan and mix well.

TOP *Tuscany Triangles* CENTRE *Cheese Gougettes* BOTTOM *Garlic Twists*

83

TOP *Vegetable Thins* BOTTOM *Chicken & Sesame Toasts*

3. Place teaspoonfuls of the mixture on greased baking sheets, allowing room to expand, and bake in the centre of the oven for 25 minutes. Cool on a wire rack.

4. Beat together the cream cheese and fromage frais until smooth; add the chives and season to taste.

5. Split the pastry puffs in half horizontally and sandwich with the cheese filling just before serving.

Makes about 45 puffs

Do not add the filling in advance, or the pastry will become soft.

CHICKEN AND SESAME TOASTS

Preparation time : 20 minutes
Cooking time : 25 minutes
Calories per slice : 348

•

10 slices of medium-cut white bread
175g (6oz) rindless streaky pork, cubed
350g (12oz) boneless chicken, skinned
1 egg white
1/2 tsp salt
1/4 tsp ground white pepper
1tsp sesame oil
75g (3oz) carrot, grated
50g (2oz) sesame seeds
oil for deep frying

1. Remove the crusts from the bread. Mince the pork and chicken or blend in a food processor until smooth. Add the egg white, salt, pepper, sesame oil and grated carrot, and mix well. Spread thickly on to the slices of bread.

2. Place the sesame seeds in a Square 1 and dip each slice of bread, meat side down, on to the seeds and press gently to coat.

3. Heat the oil in a deep fryer until a cube of bread sizzles immediately, and gently place the bread, meat side down, into the hot oil. Cook for 3 minutes. Use the Wide Spatula/Server to turn the bread and fry the other side for 2 minutes.

4. Drain and cool slightly before cutting diagonally into quarters to serve.

Makes 10 slices

The toasts can be frozen uncooked in a Freeze n Stor and then cooked straight from frozen when required.

VEGETABLE THINS

Preparation time : 20 minutes
Cooking time : 40 minutes
Calories per serving : 215

•

1/2 tsp garlic granules
1/2 tsp salt
1/2 tsp ground white pepper
1/2 tsp paprika
175g (6oz) parsnips★
225g (8oz) sweet potatoes★
175g (6oz) carrots★
150g (5oz) courgettes
1 medium unripe green plantain
oil for deep frying
(★scrubbed but not peeled)

Preheat oven to 140°C (275°F/Gas Mark 1)

1. Mix the garlic, salt, pepper and paprika in a Round 1. Set aside.

2. Slice the parsnips and sweet potatoes as thinly as possible on the Chop n Grate chopping board. Cut the carrots and courgettes diagonally into very thin slices.

3. Cut the stalk from the plantain. Using a small knife, score the skin several times along the length of the plantain. Gently but firmly ease off the skin a section at a time. Slice the plantain diagonally as thinly as possible.

4. Heat the oil until very hot and fry the prepared vegetables, a few at a time, for 2-3 minutes until slightly brown. Drain in the Colander/Server.

5. Line two baking trays with kitchen towel and place a layer of fried vegetable thins on each. Bake in the centre of the oven for 20-25 minutes, until brown and crisp. Sprinkle over the seasoning mix and serve immediately in the Party Server.

Serves 6

Spread an avocado on toast or crispbread instead of butter or margarine. It makes a delicious, healthy snack.

Colander/Server
A generous colander which drains well, and is perfect for serving salads or soft fruits. It has a wide flat base, a flow through seal and fits neatly in the serving bowls.

PRAWN AND EGG BITES

Preparation time : 25 minutes
Cooking time : 15 minutes
Calories per serving : 193-289

•

1tsp vegetable oil
3 eggs, shaken in the Quick Shake
100g (4oz) rindless streaky pork, cubed
350g (12oz) uncooked peeled prawns
50g (2oz) water chestnuts, finely chopped
3tbsp chopped fresh chives
1tsp sesame oil
1tsp salt
½ tsp ground white pepper

1. Heat the oil in a 23cm (9in) frying pan and make 3 thin omelettes, reserving a little egg for sealing the rolls.
2. Mince the pork or blend to a paste in a food processor. Mix in the prawns and the rest of the ingredients and blend for 1 minute in a food processor, until smooth.
3. Spread the mixture into a large square in the centre of each omelette, almost to the edges.
4. Fold the bottom and two side edges over the mixture, and brush the remaining flap with the reserved egg. Roll into sausage shape and seal with the flap. Place on a plate.
5. Use a steamer, or put the plate on top of an upturned bowl inside a large saucepan of boiling water. Cover and steam for 15 minutes. Leave for 5 minutes before cutting into 1cm (½ in) slices. Serve warm.

Serves 4-6

Pour hot water into the pedestal of the Serve-it-All, snap on one of the dishes and use the other as a cover. It keeps pancakes, quiches, sausage rolls etc hot for 20-30 minutes. Fill the pedestal with ice to keep things chilled.

ROQUEFORT AND PECAN CRÊPES

Preparation time : 35 minutes
Cooking time : 5 minutes
Calories per serving : 340

•

1 quantity pancake mix (page 124)
150g (5oz) Roquefort cheese
50g (2oz) pecan nuts, chopped
1tbsp chopped fresh rosemary (or 1tsp dried)
2 cloves garlic, finely chopped

Roquefort cheese comes from Aquitaine in south-western France. The cheese is made from sheeps' milk and is matured in the natural caves of the mountains of Cambalou.

freshly ground black pepper
1 egg, lightly shaken in the Quick Shake
15g (½oz) butter, melted

Preheat oven to 190°C (375°F/Gas Mark 5)

1. Make eight 20cm (8in) pancakes.
2. Place the cheese, nuts, rosemary, garlic and a little black pepper in a 1 litre Bowl, and mix thoroughly. Divide the mixture into 16 equal portions and shape each into a sausage about 5cm (2in) long.
3. Cut each pancake in half. Place a roll of cheese filling on to each and fold into a neat roll, sealing the edges with egg.
4. Place the rolls on a greased baking tray and brush with melted butter. Bake for 5 minutes in the centre of the oven. Serve hot.

Serves 4

Freeze unbaked crêpes in a Freeze n Stor. Bake from frozen for about 7 minutes.

SPICED ALMONDS

Preparation time : 30 minutes
Cooking time : 30 minutes
Calories per serving : 340

•

3tsp 5-spice powder
3 cloves garlic, crushed
2tsp star anise
1tsp ground coriander
225g (8oz) blanched almonds
4tsp salt
1tbsp vegetable oil

Preheat oven to 170°C (325°F/Gas Mark 3)

1. Place the 5-spice powder, garlic, star anise and coriander in a saucepan with 600ml (1 pint) water and bring to the boil. Cover and simmer for 10 minutes. Add the almonds and salt, return to the boil, partially cover and simmer for 15 minutes.
2. Drain through a Double Colander and discard the whole spices and garlic. Dry the almonds thoroughly, toss in oil and place on a baking sheet in a single layer. Bake for 25–30 minutes in the centre of the oven, until brown. Allow to cool thoroughly and store in an Ultra Clear Jar VII.

Serves 4

TOP *Roquefort & Pecan Crêpes* CENTRE *Prawn & Egg Bites* BOTTOM *Spiced Almonds*

TOP *Vegetable Filo Bundles* BOTTOM *Pinwheels Italiano*

VEGETABLE FILO BUNDLES

Preparation time : 45 minutes
Cooking time : 15 minutes
Calories per bundle : 22

•

1 small onion, chopped
2 cloves garlic, chopped
1tsp grated fresh ginger
75g (3oz) carrot, grated
3tbsp vegetable oil
175g (6oz) shiitake mushrooms, shredded
50g (2oz) bamboo shoots, shredded
175g (6oz) beansprouts
1/2tsp 5-spice powder
2tbsp cold water
salt and freshly ground black pepper
12 sheets filo pastry,
about 38cm x 18cm (15in x 7in)

Preheat oven to 220°C (425°F/Gas Mark 7)

1. Fry the onion, garlic, ginger and carrot in 1tbsp oil for 2 minutes over a medium heat. Add the mushrooms, bamboo shoots, beansprouts, 5-spice powder and water and cook for a further 4 minutes, stirring occasionally.
2. Adjust seasoning and transfer to a Mini Colander to drain. Allow to cool for 30 minutes.
3. Cut each pastry sheet into approximately 9cm (3 1/2 in) squares. Keep the squares wrapped up to prevent drying out. To make each bundle, layer up three squares of pastry, each lightly brushed with some of the remaining oil. Place a teaspoonful of filling in the centre, gather up the edges to make a bundle, and pinch to seal. Place the bundles on a greased baking tray and bake in the centre of the oven for 10-12 minutes, until lightly brown. Serve immediately.

Makes 32 bundles

The bundles may be frozen uncooked in a Freeze n Stor container, then baked from frozen for 15-20 minutes. You can use 75g (3oz) Chinese dried mushrooms or 175g (6oz) oyster mushrooms instead of shiitake mushrooms.

PINWHEELS ITALIANO

Preparation time : 45 minutes
Cooking time : 25 minutes
Calories per pinwheel : 61

•

225g (8oz) plain flour
75g (3oz) butter
100g (4oz) cream cheese
1tsp salt
1/4tsp ground white pepper
1tbsp chopped fresh basil
1 egg, lightly shaken in the Quick Shake
75g (3oz) sun-dried tomatoes
50g (2oz) fresh basil leaves
one 50g (1.76oz) can anchovy fillets, drained
1/2tsp mustard powder
3tbsp olive oil

Preheat oven to 200°C (400°F/Gas Mark 6)

1. Place the flour in the Multi Mixing Bowl and rub in the butter and cream cheese. Add the salt, pepper and chopped basil and mix well. Stir in the egg and press to form a dough. Seal and chill for 30 minutes.
2. Blend the remaining ingredients in a liquidiser or food processor to form a paste.
3. Roll out and trim the pastry to a rectangle about 36cm x 28cm (14in x 11in). Spread the paste evenly on the pastry, leaving a border 1cm (1/2 in) wide along the long edges. Moisten the clean edges. Cut the pastry in half lengthways. Starting with the inner edges, roll each half lengthways, ending with the moistened edge. Press to seal in the filling.
4. Cut each roll into 1cm (1/2 in) slices and place flat on greased baking sheets. Allow a little room for spreading. Bake for 20-25 minutes in the centre of the oven, until lightly brown. Cool on a wire rack.

Makes about 44 pinwheels

Sun-dried tomatoes have a unique flavour of their own, but if you cannot get them, use 3tbsp tomato purée mixed with 15g (1/2oz) fresh breadcrumbs. This will provide the right consistency, but will have a milder flavour.

Basil, an aromatic and slightly spicy herb, goes particularly well with tomatoes in any form. There are over 50 varieties of the herb, which is said to have magic properties.

5-spice powder is a mixture of star anise, Szechuan peppercorns, fennel, cloves and cinnamon. It is very strong and should be used sparingly.

When making wholemeal bread, put all dry ingredients into the Fix n Mix and shake (do not burp) to aerate without handling.

Metric Measuring Set
A compact measuring set for both liquid and dry ingredients. Dishwasher-proof and unbreakable. The cups have firm handles for scooping, while the jug has a comfortable handle and is calibrated to 500ml.

CHICKEN AND HERB TERRINE

Preparation time : 50 minutes
Chilling time : 4 hours
Calories per serving : 136

•

700g (1¹/₂ lb) boneless chicken
600ml (1 pint) chicken stock (page 126)
100g (4oz) button mushrooms, halved
75g (3oz) carrots, finely diced
1tsp chopped fresh thyme (or ¹/₂ tsp dried)
1tsp chopped fresh tarragon (or ¹/₂ tsp dried)
1tbsp chopped fresh parsley (or 1tsp dried)
1 sachet gelatine
salt and freshly ground black pepper

1. Cut the chicken into small pieces and place in saucepan with stock. Bring to the boil, cover and simmer for 15 minutes.
2. Using a Kitchen Duo Slotted Spoon remove the chicken and set to one side. Strain the stock through clean muslin and return to a clean saucepan. Add the mushrooms, carrots and herbs. Cover and simmer for 10 minutes. Remove from the heat and cool slightly.
3. Sprinkle the gelatine into the stock and stir until dissolved. Add the chicken and season to taste. Allow to cool but not set, by standing the pan in cold water for about 20 minutes.
4. Transfer the chicken mixture into the Jel n Serve, seal and refrigerate for 4 hours to set.
5. To serve, remove seal and invert mould on to the serving plate. Loosen the centre seal and gently lift off the mould.

Serves 6

The terrine should be transported in the mould for a picnic.

CUCUMBER AND MANGO SALAD

Preparation time : 15 minutes
Calories per serving : 151

•

¹/₂ cucumber, about 225g (8oz)
5 large tomatoes, skinned, quartered and seeded
1 large mango, ripe but still firm
175g (6oz) raspberries, fresh or frozen
3tbsp olive oil
1tsp Dijon mustard
3tbsp lime juice
2tsp caster sugar
salt and freshly ground black pepper

1. Cut the cucumber in half lengthways and, using a Chop n Grate, cut it into slices and place in a 1 litre Bowl with the tomatoes.
2. Peel the mango and cut down on either side of the stone, as close to the stone as possible, to give two shallow 'boats' of flesh. Remove the flesh from around the stone and cut it all into 2cm (³/₄ in) chunks. Add to the bowl.
3. Place the raspberries in a Metric Measuring Set Jug and mash with a fork. Add the remaining ingredients and mix together until a thick liquid is formed. Transfer to a Black and Clear Jug and serve with the salad.

Serves 4

ONION AND OLIVE BREAD

Preparation time : 1 hour 35 minutes
Cooking time : 30 minutes
Calories per serving : 206-309

•

150ml (5fl oz) warm water
15g (¹/₂ oz) dried yeast
50g (2oz) green olives, pitted
275g (10oz) strong bread flour
1tsp salt
3tbsp olive oil
2 medium onions, sliced
4 cloves garlic, finely chopped
1tbsp chopped fresh parsley (or 1tsp dried)

Preheat oven to 200°C (400°F/Gas Mark 6)

1. Place the water in a Metric Measuring Set Jug and sprinkle in the yeast. Leave in a warm place for about 20 minutes until frothy.
2. Quarter the olives and mix with the flour and salt in the Fix n Mix.
3. Add the yeast and 2tbsp oil to the flour and mix to form dough. Knead on a floured Pastry Sheet for 10 minutes, until

TOP *Cucumber & Mango Salad* CENTRE *Chicken & Herb Terrine* BOTTOM *Onion & Olive Bread*

91

TOP *Prawn & Rice Salad* CENTRE *Ham Mousse Baguettes* BOTTOM *Vegetable Quiche with Stilton*

elastic. Return to the Fix n Mix, seal and leave in a warm place for 30 minutes or until doubled in size.

4. Heat the remaining oil and gently fry the onion and garlic for 3 minutes. Add the parsley and leave to cool.

5. Knead the dough gently for 3 minutes and roll out to a round approximately 20cm (8in) in diameter. Transfer on to a greased baking tray and place onion mixture on top.

6. Leave in a warm place, covered with a 3 litre Bowl, for 30 minutes or until doubled in size. Bake for 30 minutes in the centre of the oven, until the onion is brown. Cool on a wire rack.

Serves 4-6

VEGETABLE QUICHE WITH STILTON

Preparation time : 1 hour 10 minutes
Cooking time : 35 minutes
Calories per serving : 454

•

1 quantity of shortcrust pastry (page 124)
225g (8oz) leeks
1tbsp vegetable oil
175g (6oz) sweetcorn
2 eggs
150ml (1/4 pint) milk
1tbsp chopped fresh thyme (or 1tsp dried)
salt and freshly ground black pepper
100g (4oz) Stilton cheese

Preheat oven to 190°C (375°F/Gas Mark 5)

1. Roll out the pastry on a Pastry Sheet to line a 20cm (8in) flan tin. Allow to rest for 30 minutes in a cool place before baking blind for 20 minutes (page 124).

2. Cut the leeks into 1cm (1/2 in) rings, wash thoroughly, and drain well. Heat the oil and fry the leeks gently for about 5 minutes until soft.

3. Place the sweetcorn and leeks in the flan case. Mix the eggs, milk, thyme and seasoning in the Quick Shake and pour into the flan case.

4. Crumble the Stilton cheese and sprinkle over the flan. Bake for approximately 35 minutes in the centre of the oven, until lightly brown.

Serves 4

HAM MOUSSE BAGUETTES

Preparation time : 25 minutes
Chilling time : 2 hours
Calories per serving : 356-474

•

2 quantities of white sauce (page 126)
2tsp gelatine
2 small baguettes
450g (1lb) lean ham
3tbsp chopped fresh parsley (or 1tbsp dried)
salt and freshly ground black pepper
100ml (4fl oz) whipping cream

1. Make the white sauce and leave to cool. Sprinkle the gelatine into 3tbsp of hot water and dissolve, using the Multi-Server (page 70).

2. Cut the baguettes in half lengthways and gently remove the centre. Finely mince the ham or blend in a food processor. Mix the ham, parsley, salt and pepper with the white sauce and add the gelatine.

3. Lightly whip the cream in a Quick Shake and fold into the ham mixture. Spoon the filling into the hollowed-out baguettes and re-form into two whole baguettes. Wrap in foil and refrigerate for 2 hours to set. To serve, cut into 2cm (3/4 in) slices.

Serves 6-8

The soft bread from the centre of the baguettes can be kept for use as breadcrumbs. Blend in a liquidiser or food processor, seal in a Freeze n Stor and freeze until required.

PRAWN AND RICE SALAD

Preparation time : 40 minutes
Calories per serving : 306-454

•

50g (2oz) wild rice
175g (6oz) long grain rice
100g (4oz) mangetout peas
3 spring onions
100g (4oz) frozen sweetcorn
350g (12oz) peeled prawns
4tbsp vegetable oil

Henry VIII gave a special award to his gardener for introducing lettuce on to the royal menu.

Pastry Sheet and Rolling Pin
The pastry sheet is printed with useful measuring guides and conversion charts. The rolling pin has a special smooth surface that does not cling to pastry. It can be filled with iced water for cooler pastry.

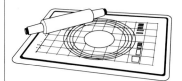

1tsp sesame oil
2tbsp white wine vinegar
1tsp coarse grain mustard
2tsp caster sugar
salt and freshly ground black pepper

1. Place the wild rice in 900ml (1¹/₂ pints) cold water and bring to the boil. Cover and simmer for 35 minutes. Refresh in cold water and drain thoroughly.

2. Cook the long grain rice in the Multi-Server (page 70). Refresh in cold water and drain thoroughly.

3. Trim the peas and cut in half crossways. Cut the spring onions into fine rings. Cook the sweetcorn and refresh in cold water, drain thoroughly.

4. Place all the rice, prawns and vegetables in a 1.5 litre Bowl.

5. Blend the remaining ingredients in the Quick Shake. Pour over the rice mixture and mix thoroughly.

Serves 4-6

SCOTCH CHICKS

Preparation time : 40 minutes
Cooking time : 20 minutes
Calories per chick : 216

•

450g (1lb) chicken breast
100g (4oz) rindless streaky bacon
1tsp salt
¹/₄ tsp ground white pepper
2tbsp chopped fresh parsley (or 2tsp dried)
¹/₂ quantity white sauce (page 126)
¹/₂ tsp hot curry powder
3 hard-boiled eggs, chopped
salt and freshly ground black pepper
1 egg, lightly shaken in the Quick Shake
100g (4oz) fresh breadcrumbs
oil for deep frying

1. Place the chicken and bacon in a food processor or mincer and mince finely.

2. Add the salt, pepper and parsley and mix thoroughly. Divide into 50g (2oz) portions and using the Hamburger Press form into thin burgers.

3. Cook the white sauce, remove from heat, and add the curry powder and

chopped eggs. Season to taste. Place a teaspoonful of egg filling in the centre of each burger and draw the edges together into a ball. Dip each one in the egg and roll in breadcrumbs.

4. Heat the oil until a cube of bread sizzles immediately and fry the chicken balls for 6 minutes, until golden brown. Serve hot or cold.

Makes about 10

SPICED ROAST BEEF

Preparation time : 10 minutes
Marinating time : 24 hours
Cooking time : 1 hour 20 minutes
Calories per serving : 429-643

•

1 medium onion, finely chopped
3 cloves garlic, crushed
1tbsp chopped fresh thyme (or 1tsp dried)
3 bay leaves
10 cloves
2tsp ground allspice
¹/₂ tsp ground black pepper
2tsp salt
450ml (³/₄ pint) red wine
3tbsp vegetable oil
1.1kg (2¹/₂ lb) beef joint, top rump

Preheat oven to 200°C (400°F/Gas Mark 6)

1. Place all the ingredients except the beef in a 4 litre Bowl.

2. Pierce the beef several times all over with a sharp fork and add to the marinade. Seal and leave for 24 hours, turning the beef every few hours.

3. Place the beef in a roasting tin, pour the marinade over, and roast for 1 hour 20 minutes, basting occasionally.

4. If to be eaten warm, allow to cool for 15 minutes before carving. Otherwise, leave to become cold before carving.

Serves 4-6

This cooking time produces a medium roast. For a rarer joint reduce the roasting time by 15 minutes. Increase the time by 15 minutes for a well-cooked joint.

For those with new babies, the Tropical Crisper can be used as a portable and liquid-tight sterilizer. Ideal for taking away on holiday.

Store left-over wine for cooking by boiling it down to half quantity and then keeping it in a Space Saver Round 2 until you need it.

TOP *Spiced Roast Beef* BOTTOM *Scotch Chicks*

TOP *Puréed Fruit Cups* CENTRE *Pear & Hazelnut Tart* BOTTOM *Mexican Chicken*

96

MEXICAN CHICKEN

Preparation time : 5 minutes
Marinating time : overnight
Cooking time : 35 minutes
Calories per serving : 203-304

•

½ medium onion, grated
2 cloves garlic, chopped
1tsp chilli powder
½ tsp ground cumin
1tsp grated fresh ginger
2tbsp paprika
2tbsp lemon juice
1tbsp vegetable oil
1tsp salt
900g (2lb) boneless chicken thighs

Preheat oven to 190°C (375°F/Gas Mark 5)

1. Place all the ingredients except the chicken in a 2 litre Bowl and mix thoroughly.
2. Add the chicken pieces and coat well. Leave overnight to marinate.
3. Transfer the chicken to a wire rack inside a roasting pan and bake for 30-35 minutes. May be eaten hot or cold.

Serves 4-6

PEAR AND HAZELNUT TART

Preparation time : 1 hour 20 minutes
Cooking time : 40 minutes
Calories per serving : 368

•

100g (4oz) plain flour
50g (2oz) butter
15g (½oz) caster sugar
100g (4oz) ground roasted hazelnuts
2 eggs
25g (1oz) self-raising flour
75g (3oz) icing sugar
50g (2oz) butter, softened
2 small ripe pears
2tbsp sieved apricot jam

Preheat oven to 190°C (375°F/Gas Mark 5)

1. Place the plain flour in a Multi Mixing Bowl and rub in the butter. Add the caster sugar and 25g (1oz) of the ground hazelnuts. Bind together with 1 egg. Seal

and refrigerate for 1 hour.
2. Roll out the pastry and line a 20cm (8in) flan tin. Leave in a cool place.
3. Place the self-raising flour, icing sugar, butter, the remaining hazelnuts and egg in a 2 litre Mix n Stor. Beat to blend thoroughly. Pour into the pastry case and smooth off.
4. Peel the pears and cut in half lengthways. Remove the core and cut each half lengthways into 5mm (¼in) slices.
5. Fan out the pear slices slightly and carefully place on to the hazelnut mixture, pressing down gently. Bake for 35-40 minutes in the centre of the oven, until brown and firm in the middle. Brush with melted apricot jam and allow to cool.

Serves 6

PURÉED FRUIT CUPS

Preparation time : 10 minutes
Calories per serving : 63/100/63

•

Pineapple and Passion Fruit:
1 medium pineapple, ripe
2 passion fruit
50g (2oz) caster sugar

1. Peel the pineapple, making sure all the 'eyelets' are removed. Cut into quarters. Remove the centre core and cut into large chunks. Place in a liquidiser or food processor with the sugar and blend until smooth. Cut the passion fruit in half, scoop out the flesh and add to the pineapple. Mix thoroughly and transfer to a 1 litre Picnic Jug. Add 10 ice cubes and seal until required.
2. To serve, dilute with lemonade or sparkling water to taste. As a guide, use two thirds juice to one third lemonade or water.

Each jug will serve four.

Variations: *Pear and Mango* - 2 medium ripe pears, 1 large ripe mango, 50g (2oz) caster sugar.
Strawberry and Lime - 225g (8oz) strawberries, juice of 2 limes, 50g (2oz) caster sugar.

The leaves on a ripe pineapple should be slightly withered, the skin a deep yellow, and the fruit should smell rich and fragrant.

1 Litre Picnic Jug
A sturdy practical size for juices, squashes or milk. Spillproof for travelling and picnics.

10
Barbecues

The cooking times in this section refer to grilling rather than barbecuing, as the latter is often unpredictable.

Hamburger Press
Make your own hamburgers or chicken burgers, simply and easily with wholesome ingredients. A delicious alternative to 'shop-bought'!

CITRUS CHICKEN

Preparation time : 10 minutes
Marinating time : 6 hours
Cooking time : 30 minutes
Calories per serving : 235

•

1 small lemon
1 lime
$^1/_2$ orange
1tbsp walnut oil
$^1/_2$ medium onion, grated
4tbsp chopped fresh parsley
1tsp mustard powder
1tbsp soft brown sugar
$^1/_2$ tsp salt and freshly ground black pepper
4 chicken breasts on the bone,
about 175g (6oz) each

1. Using the Cook's Maid, remove the zest and juice of the lemon, lime and orange. Place juice and zest in a 3 litre Bowl and mix thoroughly with the rest of the ingredients, except for the chicken.
2. Cut shallow slashes across the chicken breasts and add to the marinade. Mix thoroughly, seal and leave for 6 hours or overnight.
3. Either barbecue or place on a rack under a preheated, medium hot grill for 15 minutes each side, until golden brown and cooked through.

Serves 4

VEGGIE BURGERS

Preparation time : 30 minutes
Chilling time : 2 hours
Cooking time : 15 minutes
Calories per serving : 266

•

1tbsp vegetable oil
1 medium onion, finely chopped
2 cloves garlic, finely chopped
50g (2oz) button mushrooms, chopped
225g (8oz) boiled potatoes, mashed
50g (2oz) sesame seeds, toasted
50g (2oz) sunflower seeds
100g (4oz) carrot, grated
100g (4oz) parsnip, grated
salt and freshly ground black pepper
1 egg, lightly shaken in the Quick Shake

1. Heat the oil and gently fry the onion and garlic for 5 minutes until just starting to brown. Add the mushrooms and continue frying for 2 minutes.
2. Place the mashed potato in a 3 litre Bowl and add to it the onion mixture, sesame and sunflower seeds, carrot, parsnip, salt and pepper. Mix well together and then add the egg.
3. Use the Hamburger Press to form 8 burgers, and refrigerate for 2 hours.
4. With great care these burgers can be barbecued. However, it is easier to heat up a little oil in a frying pan and fry the burgers for 4 minutes on each side, until golden brown.

Serves 4

Serve with homemade tomato sauce (see Tomato Fish Balls, page 118).

PORK IN PEPPER MARINADE

Preparation time : 5 minutes
Marinating time : 6 hours
Cooking time : 14 minutes
Calories per serving : 534

•

2tbsp black peppercorns
2 cloves garlic, finely chopped
2tbsp white wine vinegar
4tbsp olive oil
1tsp salt
4 pork chops, about 175g (6oz) each

1. Crush the peppercorns in a pestle and mortar, or place inside a strong plastic bag and hit with a hammer. Place the crushed peppercorns in a 3 litre Bowl and mix with the rest of the ingredients, except for the pork.
2. Add the pork to the marinade and mix until well coated. Seal and chill for 6 hours or overnight.
3. Barbecue or place on a rack and cook for 7 minutes each side under a preheated hot grill, turning with a Fork/Slim Spatula.

Serves 4

This marinade is also excellent with steak.

TOP LEFT *Citrus Chicken* TOP RIGHT *Pork in Pepper Marinade* BOTTOM *Veggie Burgers*

TOP *Lamb Cutlets with Yogurt & Herbs* CENTRE *Chinese Barbecue Pork* BOTTOM *Tropical Fruit Kebabs*

TROPICAL FRUIT KEBABS

Preparation time : 30 minutes
Marinating time : 2 hours
Cooking time : 8 minutes
Calories per serving : 160

•

1 star fruit
1/2 medium pineapple
1 mango
1/2 pawpaw
1 lime
1/2 orange
4tbsp chopped fresh mint
2tbsp hazelnut oil
1tbsp soft brown sugar
150ml (1/4 pint) plain yogurt

1. Cut the star fruit into 1cm (1/2 in) slices and then cut each slice in half. Peel and cut the pineapple, mango and pawpaw into large chunks. Place in a 2 litre Bowl.
2. Use the Cook's Maid to remove the zest and juice from the lime and orange. Mix with the mint, oil and brown sugar, and pour over the fruit. Gently toss the fruit in the marinade to coat, seal and leave in a cool place for 2 hours (no longer, otherwise the fruit will be too soft to barbecue).
3. Divide the fruit between 8 pre-soaked wooden skewers and barbecue until bubbling and slightly brown. If grilling, place the kebabs on a rack and cook under a preheated hot grill for 4 minutes each side. Serve immediately with plain yogurt.

Serves 4

Any type of firm fruit is suitable - just use what is available.

LAMB CUTLETS WITH YOGURT AND HERBS

Preparation time : 5 minutes
Marinating time : 4 hours
Cooking time : 14 minutes
Calories per serving : 510

•

150ml (1/4 pint) plain yogurt
1tbsp chopped fresh rosemary (or 1tsp dried)
2tbsp chopped fresh mint (or 2tsp dried)
1 clove garlic, finely chopped

1tsp whole grain mustard
1/2 tsp salt and freshly ground black pepper
8 lamb cutlets, about 100g-175g (4oz-6oz) each

1. Mix all the ingredients except the lamb cutlets in a 3 litre Bowl. Add the lamb, and mix thoroughly to coat. Seal and refrigerate for at least 4 hours.
2. Barbecue until brown on both sides. If using the grill, heat to high, place the lamb on a rack and grill for 7 minutes on each side until lightly browned.

Serves 4

CHINESE BARBECUE PORK

Preparation time : 10 minutes
Marinating time : 6 hours
Cooking time : 30 minutes
Calories per serving : 297-446

•

1tbsp grated fresh ginger
3 cloves garlic, crushed
2tbsp barbecue or Hoi Sin sauce
1tbsp crushed yellow bean sauce
1/4 tsp ground white pepper
2tsp soft brown sugar
1/2 tsp 5-spice powder
1tbsp sesame oil
700g (11/2 lb) pork fillet

1. Mix all the ingredients except the pork in a 3 litre Bowl.
2. Cut the pork fillet in half and add to the marinade mixture, coating thoroughly. Seal and chill for at least 6 hours, or overnight if possible, to ensure maximum flavour.
3. Cook slowly on the barbecue, turning frequently to prevent burning. If grilling, preheat the grill to medium hot, place the pork on a rack and grill for 10-15 minutes on each side, until cooked thoroughly. Let the meat cool slightly before cutting it into thin slices to serve.

Serves 4 to 6

If you have to 'feed' a barbecue while you're cooking, push the hot embers to the middle and the new fuel to the edges.

Soaking the wooden skewers before use prevents them burning on the barbecue.

Don't salt food before you grill it as this will draw out the juices.

CHICKEN SATAY WITH PEANUT SAUCE

Preparation time : 10 minutes
Marinating time : 4 hours
Cooking time : 20 minutes
Calories per serving : 473

•

2 cloves garlic, finely chopped
2tbsp chopped fresh coriander
1tbsp tahini (sesame paste)
3tbsp vegetable oil
3tbsp dark soy sauce
700g (1¹/₂lb) boneless chicken thighs
1tbsp vegetable oil
¹/₂ medium onion, grated
1 clove garlic, finely chopped
4tbsp crunchy peanut butter
2tbsp tahini (sesame paste)
¹/₂tsp chilli powder
1tbsp soft brown sugar
150ml (¹/₄ pint) water
2tsp dark soy sauce
1tbsp freshly squeezed lime juice

1. Mix the first 5 ingredients together in a 2 litre Bowl. Cut the chicken into strips approximately 2.5cm x 5cm (1in x 2in) and add to the marinade. Mix thoroughly, seal and chill for 4 hours.
2. To make the sauce, heat the oil and fry the onion and garlic gently for 5 minutes. Add the peanut butter, tahini and chilli powder. Cook for a further 3 minutes. Add the remaining ingredients, stirring until the sauce is creamy and just starting to thicken. Remove from heat and pour into an Oriental Twin.
3. Thread the chicken strips, concertina-fashion, on to 12 pre-soaked wooden skewers, and barbecue. If using the grill, place on a rack and cook under high heat for 5 minutes each side. Serve hot with the peanut sauce.

Serves 4

Pork works equally well marinated and cooked this way.

MONKFISH KEBABS WITH PIQUANT SAUCE

Preparation time : 10 minutes
Marinating time : 2 hours
Cooking time : 10 minutes
Calories per serving : 372

•

2tbsp white wine vinegar
3tbsp hazelnut oil
1tsp whole grain mustard
1tsp chopped fresh dill (or ¹/₄ tsp dried)
1tsp chopped fresh tarragon (or ¹/₂ tsp dried)
¹/₂ tsp salt and freshly ground black pepper
700g (1¹/₂lb) monkfish
8 dried peaches, cut in half
50g (2oz) fresh parsley
1tsp coarse grain mustard
15g (¹/₂ oz) capers
3tbsp olive oil
1tbsp freshly squeezed lime juice
2tsp caster sugar (optional)
salt and freshly ground black pepper

1. Mix the first 6 ingredients together in a 2 litre Bowl. Cut the monkfish into large chunks and add to the marinade, with the dried peaches. Seal and leave for at least 2 hours.
2. Blend the parsley, mustard, capers, oil, lime juice and sugar in a liquidiser or food processor for 1 minute. Season to taste and blend for a further 15 seconds. Transfer the sauce into a bowl from the Table Mates Set; cover and leave at room temperature to serve with the kebabs.
3. Thread monkfish and peaches alternately on to 8 pre-soaked wooden skewers. Barbecue, or cook under a preheated grill on a high setting for 10 minutes, turning to brown evenly.

Serves 4

Try using other types of firm fish, or shellfish such as prawns or scallops.

Wrap whole fish in vine leaves before barbecuing. Not only do the leaves impart flavour and keep the fish moist, but when they are peeled back the fish skin comes away too.

Kitchen Duo Fork/Slim Spatula
Can be fastened in two ways, to provide the exact 'grip' needed for turning kebabs, sausages, or other barbecue food. The Duos are strong, break-resistant, and easy to use.

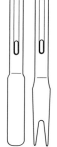

TOP *Chicken Satay with Peanut Sauce* BOTTOM *Monkfish Kebabs with Piquant Sauce*

103

Keep 1½kg (3lb) flour and 700g (1½lb) margarine mixed to breadcrumb stage in the Fix n Mix. Draw off smaller quantities as required. Add salt for savoury pastry, sugar for sweet, and currants and sugar for fruit scones.

Jel n Serve
Just the right size for most mousses, moulds, jellies or desserts. Comes with its own seal for safe storage in the fridge.

COCONUT YEAST CAKE

Preparation time : 30 minutes
Resting time : 1 hour 20 minutes
Cooking time : 30 minutes
Calories in total : 1626

•

150ml (5fl oz) warm milk
15g (½oz) dried yeast
275g (10oz) strong bread flour
25g (1oz) butter
50g (2oz) caster sugar
2 egg yolks
50g (2oz) caster sugar
75g (3oz) desiccated coconut

Preheat oven to 190°C (375°F/Gas Mark 5)

1. Place the warm milk in the Metric Measuring Set Jug, sprinkle in the dried yeast, and leave in a warm place to become frothy (about 20 minutes).
2. Using the Sift n Stor, sieve the flour into the Fix n Mix, rub in the butter and stir in the sugar. Add the yeast mixture and mix with a Paddle Scraper until a dough forms.
3. Turn the dough out on to a Pastry Sheet, lightly dust with flour and knead for 10 minutes, until soft and smooth.
4. Return the dough to the Fix n Mix, seal and leave in a warm place for 30 minutes or until doubled in size. Meanwhile grease an 18cm (7in) cake tin and line the bottom with baking parchment.
5. Gently knead the dough for 3 minutes and then roll out to a rectangle approximately 40cm x 23cm (16in x 9in), using the measurements at the side of the Pastry Sheet as a guide.
6. Place the egg yolks and remaining sugar in a 1 litre Mix n Stor and, using an electric whisk, beat until pale and stiff. Stir in the desiccated coconut and spread on to the rolled-out dough, spreading to almost the edge on the shorter sides and to within 4cm (1½in) of the edge on the long sides.
7. Gently roll up the dough from the long side, finishing with the end underneath. Slice the roll into 8 equal pieces and place in the cake tin with the cut sides uppermost. Place the tin inside the Fix n Mix, seal and leave in a warm place for 30

minutes, or until doubled in size.
8. Bake for 20-25 minutes in the centre of the oven, until golden brown. Turn out on to a rack to cool.

This cake is best eaten on the day it is cooked, but any leftovers will freeze well.

ROCKY ROAD GÂTEAU

Preparation time : 20 minutes
Chilling time : 4 hours
Calories in total : 4450

•

175g (6oz) plain chocolate
3tbsp strong black coffee
350g (12oz) Hob-nob biscuits
100g (4oz) marshmallows
100g (4oz) roasted hazelnuts, chopped
100g (4oz) glacé cherries, quartered
25g (1oz) desiccated coconut
4tbsp single cream
150ml (¼ pint) whipped cream
about 25g (1oz) roasted whole hazelnuts
for decoration

1. Place the chocolate and coffee in a Tropical Salad Bowl and melt the chocolate in a Multi-Server (page 70).
2. Put the biscuits in a strong polythene bag and use the Rolling Pin to crush them into small pieces. Place in a Multi Mixing Bowl. With a pair of scissors, cut the marshmallows into small pieces and add to the bowl with the chopped hazelnuts, cherries and coconut, mixing thoroughly.
3. Stir the melted chocolate until smooth and add the single cream, stirring until well blended. Pour into the biscuit mixture and mix thoroughly.
4. Transfer the biscuit mixture into a Jel n Serve, pressing down lightly. Refrigerate for 4 hours to set.
5. Loosen the cake by dipping the mould into boiling water for a slow count of 5. Remove the seal and put the serving plate in its place. Turn it upside down and remove the centre seal. Carefully lift off the ring and allow the cake to drop on to the plate.
6. To decorate, pipe rosettes of whipped cream on the top and around the base, and top with whole hazelnuts.

TOP *Rocky Road Gâteau* BOTTOM *Coconut Yeast Cake*

TOP *Oaty Banana Curls* CENTRE *Coffee & Almond Shorties* BOTTOM *Apricot & Cherry Cookies*

OATY BANANA CURLS

Preparation time : 15 minutes
Cooking time : 30 minutes
Calories per biscuit : 100

100g (4oz) unsalted butter
100g (4oz) soft brown sugar
4tbsp golden syrup
50g (2oz) porridge oats
50g (2oz) plain flour
50g (2oz) dried banana chips, finely crushed

Preheat oven to 170°C (325°F/Gas Mark 3)

1. Place the butter, sugar and syrup in a large saucepan and cook over a medium heat, stirring, until the sugar has dissolved and the mixture is well blended. Allow to cool for 5 minutes. Add the porridge oats, flour and banana chips and mix well.
2. Place teaspoonfuls of mixture on to baking trays lined with silicon baking parchment. Allow plenty of room for the mixture to spread.
3. Bake for 13-15 minutes in the centre of the oven until bubbling and golden brown. (Be very careful because the biscuits will remain soft if they are undercooked but will burn if overcooked.)
4. Cool for 3-4 minutes until almost set, then roll each biscuit around the handle of a wooden spoon. Allow to cool completely on a wire rack.
5. Store in a Space Saver Rectangle.

Makes 20-24 curls

These curls must be stored airtight or they will become soft and sticky.

APRICOT AND CHERRY COOKIES

Preparation time : 15 minutes
Cooking time : 24 minutes
Calories per biscuit : 114

75g (3oz) glacé cherries
100g (4oz) dried apricots
150g (5oz) plain flour
1/2 tsp baking powder
100g (4oz) unsalted butter, softened
150g (5oz) caster sugar
1 egg

Preheat oven to 190°C (375°F/Gas Mark 5)

1. Cut the cherries into quarters, then rinse in cold water to remove any syrup; dry thoroughly. Cut the apricots into small pieces.
2. Place the flour and baking powder in a Sift n Stor. Beat the butter and sugar together in a Multi Mixing Bowl until light and fluffy. Add the egg, sift in the flour and beat until well combined.
3. Stir in the cherries and apricots until well distributed. Place teaspoonfuls of the mixture on to greased baking trays, allowing room to spread, and bake for 10-12 minutes in the centre of the oven, until pale brown.
4. Leave to stand for 3 minutes before transferring to a cooling rack. Store in an Ultra Clear Jar VI.

Makes 20-24 cookies

These cookies are slightly soft and after storage may be reheated in the oven for a 'just-baked' taste.

COFFEE AND ALMOND SHORTIES

Preparation time : 30 minutes
Cooking time : 25 minutes
Calories per biscuit : 86

100g (4oz) plain flour
2tsp instant coffee powder
100g (4oz) unsalted butter, softened
50g (2oz) caster sugar
50g (2oz) ground almonds
1 egg, shaken in the Quick Shake
15g (1/2oz) flaked almonds

Preheat oven to 150°C (300°F/Gas Mark 2)

1. Place the flour and coffee powder in a Sift n Stor, seal and shake to mix.
2. In a Multi Mixing Bowl, beat the butter and sugar till pale in colour, and sift in the flour mixture. Add the ground almonds, stir thoroughly, then press together into a dough. Seal and chill for 45 minutes before rolling out.
3. Lightly dust a Rolling Pin and Pastry Sheet with flour and roll out the dough to

For decorating cakes, puddings, Christmas trees or children's party bags, melt cooking chocolate and pour into the seal shapes from the Jel n Serve or the animal shapes of the Noah's Ark. Use sultanas or cherries for eyes etc.

Keep a vanilla pod in sugar to be used in cakes and desserts. If using vanilla extract, avoid using synthetic varieties.

5mm (¹/₄ in) thick. Use a 6.5cm Cookie Cutter to cut out the biscuits. Re-roll the trimmings.

4. Place the biscuits on ungreased baking trays, allowing a little room to spread. Brush with egg and press a few flaked almonds on top. Bake for 20-25 minutes in the centre of the oven, until pale brown. Cool on the baking tray for 5 minutes before transferring to a wire rack. Store in an Ultra Clear Jar VI.

Makes 18-20 biscuits

RASPBERRY CORNMEAL MUFFINS

Preparation time : 10 minutes
Cooking time : 25 minutes
Calories per muffin : 125

•

175g (6oz) self-raising flour
3tsp baking powder
175g (6oz) cornmeal
50g (2oz) unsalted butter
100g (4oz) caster sugar
50g (2oz) walnuts, chopped
1 egg, lightly shaken in the Quick Shake
300ml (¹/₂ pint) raspberry yogurt
175g (6oz) fresh raspberries

Preheat oven to 190°C (375°F/Gas Mark 5)

1. Using the Sift n Stor, sieve the flour, baking powder and cornmeal into a Multi Mixing Bowl. Rub in the butter and add the sugar and chopped walnuts.
2. Stir in the egg and yogurt until well mixed, and then carefully fold in the raspberries.
3. Line deep bun tins with paper cases and fill each three-quarters full with the muffin mixture. Bake for 25 minutes in the centre of the oven, until firm and golden brown.

Makes 20-24 muffins

When in season, other fruit can also be used; for example, blueberries. Just match the flavour of the yogurt as appropriate.

CHOCOLATE ORANGE CAKE

Preparation time : 15 minutes
Cooking time : 30 minutes
Cooling time : 45 minutes
Calories in total : 2340

•

100g (4oz) self-raising flour
1tsp baking powder
15g (¹/₂oz) cocoa powder
100g (4oz) caster sugar
100g (4oz) soft margarine
2 eggs, lightly shaken in the Quick Shake
zest of 1 large orange, using the Cook's Maid
3tbsp orange juice
100g (4oz) white chocolate
100ml (4fl oz) fromage frais

Preheat oven to 180°C (350°F/Gas Mark 4)

1. Grease and line the base of two 18cm (7in) sponge tins with baking parchment.
2. Using the Sift n Stor, sieve the flour, baking powder, cocoa powder and sugar into the Multi Mixing Bowl. Add the margarine, eggs, orange zest and 1tbsp of the juice, and whisk until thoroughly combined (an electric whisk is ideal).
3. Divide the mixture evenly between the tins, level off and bake for 20-25 minutes in the centre of the oven, until the cake springs back up when gently pressed. Leave for 1 minute before turning out on to a rack to cool.
4. To make the cream filling, place the chocolate and remaining juice in a Tropical Salad Bowl and melt the chocolate using the Multi-Server (page 70). Stir until smooth and then mix in the fromage frais. Chill the mixture in the fridge for about half an hour, until it resembles whipped cream.
5. Peel the paper from the cakes and use one third of the chocolate cream to sandwich the cakes together. Place the cake on the base of a Domed Server and spread another third of the cream on the top. Place the remaining chocolate cream in a piping bag fitted with a star nozzle and pipe rosettes around the edge. Store in the Domed Server – it will keep for several days.

To rescue a cake with a sunken middle, cut out the middle section and transform it into a ring.

Ultra Clear Jar
Keep those special biscuits and cookies really fresh in the airtight and elegant Ultra Clear Jar VI. Made of a very clear translucent material, it's attractive and unbreakable too.

TOP *Raspberry Cornmeal Muffins* BOTTOM *Chocolate Orange Cake*

LEFT *Double Chocolate & Peach Cookies* TOP RIGHT *Hazelnut & Apple Crumble Cake* BOTTOM *Lemon Seed Cake*

DOUBLE CHOCOLATE AND PEACH COOKIES

Preparation time : 15 minutes
Cooking time : 30 minutes
Calories per biscuit : 141

·

100g (4oz) plain flour
25g (1oz) cocoa powder
¹/₂ tsp baking powder
100g (4oz) unsalted butter, softened
100g (4oz) soft brown sugar
1 egg
175g (6oz) white chocolate, broken into small chunks
100g (4oz) dried peaches, chopped

Preheat oven to 190°C (375°F/Gas Mark 5)

1. Use the Sift n Stor to measure the flour, cocoa powder and baking powder.
2. Place the butter, sugar and egg in a 2 litre Mix n Stor and whisk until well blended. Sieve in the flour mixture, then add the chocolate and peaches. Mix well.
3. Place teaspoonfuls of the mixture on to greased baking trays, leaving plenty of room to spread. Bake for 12-15 minutes in the centre of the oven.
4. Cool slightly before transferring to wire racks to cool further.

Makes 20-24 cookies

LEMON SEED CAKE

Preparation time : 15 minutes
Cooking time : 50 minutes
Calories in total : 3008

·

2 large lemons
175g (6oz) unsalted butter, softened
175g (6oz) caster sugar
3 eggs, shaken in the Quick Shake
225g (8oz) self-raising flour
25g (1oz) caraway seeds
25g (1oz) poppy seeds

Preheat oven to 170°C (325°F/Gas Mark 3)

1. Grease a 1.5 litre (2¹/₂ pint) loaf tin and line the bottom with baking parchment. Using a Cook's Maid, remove the zest and juice from the lemons; set to one side.

2. Place the butter and sugar in a Multi Mixing Bowl and whisk until light and fluffy.
3. Whisk in the eggs in 4 stages, ensuring that it is thoroughly mixed before adding the next batch. Fold in the flour.
4. Mix the caraway and poppy seeds and gently stir into the mixture. Finally stir in the lemon juice and zest and transfer to the prepared loaf tin.
5. Bake for 50 minutes in the centre of the oven, or until brown and the cake feels firm in the middle. Leave for 10 minutes before turning out to cool on a wire rack.

Orange can also be used instead of lemons. Just substitute the juice and zest of 1 medium orange.

HAZELNUT AND APPLE CRUMBLE CAKE

Preparation time : 20 minutes
Cooking time : 1 hour
Calories in total : 2656

·

275g (10oz) Bramley apples, peeled and chopped
4tbsp cold water
25g (1oz) unsalted butter
25g (1oz) plain flour
25g (1oz) hazelnuts, chopped
25g (1oz) caster sugar
175g (6oz) self-raising flour
¹/₂ tsp baking powder
100g (4oz) soft margarine
100g (4oz) caster sugar
2 eggs
50g (2oz) roasted hazelnuts, chopped

Preheat oven to 170°C (325°F/Gas Mark 3)

1. Gently cook the apples and water in a saucepan, until thick but still lumpy. Leave to cool.
2. To make the crumble, rub the butter into the plain flour in a Multi Mixing Bowl, add the chopped hazelnuts and sugar, mix and transfer to a small bowl. Grease an 18cm (7in) loose bottom cake tin and line the bottom with baking parchment.

To pretty-up a plain cake in seconds, put a paper doily on top like a template and sift icing sugar over it. Remove the doily carefully to reveal an instant decoration.

To cut down on sugar when cooking soft fruits, add a pinch of bicarbonate of soda.

3. Use a Sift n Stor to sieve the self raising flour and baking powder into the Multi Mixing Bowl. Add the margarine, the remaining sugar and the eggs, and beat until well mixed. Gently stir in the apple sauce and roasted hazelnuts, and transfer the mixture into the prepared cake tin. Smooth the mixture and sprinkle the crumble over. Bake for 1 hour in the centre of the oven, until the topping is pale golden.

4. Leave for 5 minutes before removing from the tin, and cool on a wire rack.

ALMOND AND SWEETCORN CAKE

Preparation time : 15 minutes
Cooking time : 1 hour 5 minutes
Calories in total : 3800

.

225g (8oz) self-raising flour
1tsp baking powder
100g (4oz) ground almonds
175g (6oz) unsalted butter, softened
175g (6oz) caster sugar
2 eggs, lightly shaken in a Quick Shake
one 298g (10¹/₂oz) can creamed sweetcorn
¹/₂ tsp almond essence
25g (1oz) flaked almonds

Preheat oven to 170°C (325°F/Gas Mark 3)

1. Using the Sift n Stor, sieve the flour and baking powder into a 1 litre Bowl and add the ground almonds. Grease a 20cm (8in) cake tin and line the bottom with baking parchment.

2. Beat the butter and sugar together until pale and fluffy, and gradually beat in the eggs.

3. Alternately fold in the flour mixture and creamed sweetcorn in three stages, and finally add the almond essence.

4. Transfer to the cake tin, smooth the top and sprinkle on the flaked almonds. Bake for 65 minutes in the centre of the oven, until the middle of the cake is firm when pressed. Leave for 10 minutes before turning out to cool on a wire rack.

You can freeze nuts in their shells for up to a year if you put them in Freeze n Stor containers.

Try using carob as a substitute for chocolate in cakes and desserts. It has a slightly different flavour but is equally delicious.

PECAN BROWNIES

Preparation time : 20 minutes
Cooking time : 25 minutes
Calories per brownie : 240

.

75g (3oz) plain chocolate
100g (4oz) unsalted butter
2 eggs
175g (6oz) soft brown sugar
4tbsp Greek yogurt
75g (3oz) plain flour
100g (4oz) pecan nuts, chopped

Preheat oven to 170°C (325°F/Gas Mark 3)

1. Place the chocolate and butter in a Tropical Salad Bowl and melt in the Multi-Server (page 70). Grease a tin 25cm x 18cm (10in x 7in), line with baking parchment and set to one side.

2. Beat the eggs and sugar in a 2 litre Mix n Stor until light and fluffy; slowly beat in the chocolate mixture and yogurt, until well blended. Gently fold in the flour and pecan nuts and transfer to the prepared tin. Smooth the top and bake for 25 minutes in the centre of the oven, until the middle of the cake is firm to touch.

3. Leave to cool in the tin before cutting into 12 squares. Store in a Rectangle 1.

Makes 12

These delicious brownies may be topped with a chocolate frosting for an even more chocolatey taste. Melt 100g (4oz) plain chocolate and beat in 100g (4oz) cream cheese or low-fat cream cheese. When thoroughly blended, spread over the cake and allow to set slightly before cutting into squares.

TOP *Almond & Sweetcorn Cake* BOTTOM *Pecan Brownies*

12
Children's Parties

It is false economy to buy a milder, cheaper Cheddar for cooking as you will need a lot of it to create a strong flavour. You are better off using a smaller amount of a stronger-tasting, more expensive variety.

Cookie Cutters
A delightful set of five cleverly designed cutters nesting in their own neat case. Provides all the shapes that you are ever likely to need for pastries and biscuits. Children love them!

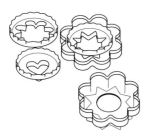

ALPHABET PASTRIES

Preparation time : 1 hour
Cooking time : 20 minutes
Calories per pastry : 100

•

225g (8oz) plain flour
1/4 tsp salt
100g (4oz) butter
2tbsp chopped fresh parsley (or 2tsp dried)
175g (6oz) Cheddar cheese, grated
75g (3oz) red eating apple
50g (2oz) sweetcorn
1tbsp chopped fresh chives (optional)
1 egg yolk, lightly beaten

Preheat oven to 190°C (375°F/Gas Mark 5)

1. Place the flour and salt in a Multi Mixing Bowl and rub in the butter. Add the parsley and half the grated cheese, and bind together with 2tbsp cold water. Seal and refrigerate for 30 minutes.
2. Core but do not peel the apple and chop finely. Place in a 1 litre Bowl with the sweetcorn, the remaining cheese and chives (if used). Mix together.
3. Roll out the pastry on a floured Pastry Sheet until 3mm (1/8 in) thick. Cut out 24 discs using the large 8cm Cookie Cutter. Trimmings may be pressed together and rolled out again. Place a teaspoonful of apple filling in the centre of each pastry disc, brush the edge with cold water, and fold in half. Press the edges with a fork to seal, and pierce a hole for steam.
4. Cut out the initials of each child from the pastry trimmings and stick on to the pastries with a little water. Brush lightly with egg yolk and bake for 20 minutes in the centre of the oven, until pale brown. The pastries may be eaten hot or cold.

Makes 24

CHERRY AND HONEY MINI DROP SCONES

Preparation time : 10 minutes
Cooking time : 40 minutes
Calories per scone : 19

•

150g (5oz) plain flour
1/2 tsp baking powder
100g (4oz) glacé cherries
1 egg
3tbsp clear honey
150ml (1/4 pint) milk
1tbsp vegetable oil for frying

1. Use the Sift n Stor to sieve the flour and baking powder together into a Multi Mixing Bowl.
2. Chop the cherries into small pieces, rinse in cold water to remove all the syrup, and dry thoroughly. Then add to the flour. Add the egg, honey and milk, and stir until well mixed.
3. Lightly grease a large frying pan and cook teaspoonfuls of the mixture over a medium heat for about 2 minutes, until the top starts to set. Using a Kitchen Duo Slim Spatula, turn the scones over and fry the other side for 2 minutes, until brown. Cool on a wire rack. Store and serve the scones in a Cheese Tray.

Makes approximately 60

Cooked drop scones can be frozen in a Freeze n Stor.

FRANKFURTER SPIRALS

Preparation time : 45 minutes
Cooking time : 20 minutes
Calories per spiral : 95

•

100g (4oz) plain wholemeal flour
1/4 tsp salt
50g (2oz) butter
50g (2oz) cream cheese
12 frankfurters, halved
1 egg, lightly shaken in the Quick Shake
15g (1/2 oz) poppy seeds

Preheat oven to 190°C (375°F/Gas Mark 5)

1. Place the flour and salt in a Multi Mixing Bowl and rub in the butter and cream cheese. Bind together with 2tbsp of cold water, pressing together to form a dough. Seal and refrigerate for 30 minutes.
2. Lightly dust the Pastry Sheet, roll out and trim the pastry to 30cm x 15cm (12in x

TOP *Alphabet Pastries* CENTRE *Frankfurter Spirals* BOTTOM *Cherry & Honey Mini Drop Scones*

LEFT *Animal Sarnies* RIGHT *Apple & Currant Pixie Scones*

6in). Cut the rectangle into 24 strips measuring 15cm x 1cm (6in x ½ in). Wrap each strip around the frankfurter halves in a spiral fashion.

3. Place each spiral on a baking sheet with the ends of the pastry underneath. Brush with egg, sprinkle poppy seeds over, and bake in the centre of the oven for 20 minutes. Serve hot or cold.

Makes 24 spirals

APPLE AND CURRANT PIXIE SCONES

Preparation time : 25 minutes
Cooking time : 10 minutes
Calories per scone : 42
•

225g (8oz) self-raising flour
1tsp ground cinnamon
1tsp baking powder
50g (2oz) unsalted butter
2 small Golden Delicious apples
100g (4oz) currants
50g (2oz) caster sugar
2tbsp plain yogurt

Preheat oven to 200°C (400°F/Gas Mark 6)

1. Sieve together the flour, cinnamon and baking powder into a Multi Mixing Bowl and rub in the butter.
2. Peel and grate the apples and add, with the currants and sugar, to the flour mixture. Add the yogurt and mix to a soft dough.
3. Dust a Pastry Sheet with flour and roll the dough out until 1cm (½ in) thick. Cut out hearts or stars with the Cookie Cutters, or cut small triangles and squares with a knife. Trimmings can be gathered up and re-rolled for more shapes.
4. Place on a greased baking tray and bake in the centre of the oven for 10 minutes until pale brown. Cool on a wire rack.

Makes approximately 40

Children can help make the scones using their own Mini Mix-It Set.

ANIMAL SARNIES

Preparation time : 2 hours
Calories per sandwich : 64-70
1•
2 hard-boiled eggs, chopped
2tbsp mayonnaise
1tbsp chopped fresh chives (optional)
2•
50g (2oz) cream cheese
1tbsp fromage frais
50g (2oz) ham, finely chopped
50g (2oz) pineapple, cut into small pieces
3•
25g (1oz) cooked sweetcorn
25g (1oz) cooked petit pois
75g (3oz) boiled potato, finely chopped
2tbsp mayonnaise
4•
175g (6oz) ripe banana, mashed
1tbsp fromage frais
50g (2oz) dates, chopped

1 large thin-sliced brown loaf
1 large thin-sliced white loaf

Make up the four fillings separately as follows:

1. Mix together the eggs, mayonnaise and chives (if used).
2. Beat the cream cheese and fromage frais together, and mix in the ham and pineapple.
3. Blend the sweetcorn and peas in a liquidiser or food processor until lightly chopped. Mix with the potatoes and mayonnaise.
4. Mix together the banana, fromage frais and dates.
5. Using the hollow half of the Animals from the Noah's Ark, cut out shapes from the bread. You do this by placing 2 animal shapes on top of a slice of bread and rolling over firmly with the Rolling Pin. Sandwich pairs of animals together with the fillings. Match the animal shapes to the fillings - eg white polar bears filled with egg mayonnaise; lions filled with ham and pineapple; etc.

Makes 48 sandwiches

The frankfurter originated in the small German town of Neuisenburg near Frankfurt, and through the invention of the American hot dog became the world's best-known sausage. The genuine article is made from prime lean pork and a little salted bacon fat, but the Anglo-American version is usually pork and beef, and sometimes beef on its own.

Tupperware products have been awarded the Certificate of the Royal Institute of Public Health and Hygiene every year since 1965.

TOMATO FISH BALLS

Preparation time : 35 minutes
Cooking time : 15 minutes
Calories per fish ball : 18

•

450g (1lb) skinless cod fillet
2 egg whites
1tsp salt
¼ tsp ground white pepper
50g (2oz) carrot, grated
3tbsp chopped fresh chives (or 1tbsp dried)
2tbsp cornflour
1 medium onion, finely chopped
1tbsp vegetable oil
one 397g (14oz) can chopped tomatoes
1tbsp tomato purée
1tsp red wine vinegar
25g (1oz) soft brown sugar
4 large fresh basil leaves (optional)

1. Remove any small bones from the fish, then finely mince or blend in a food processor until smooth. Place in a Multi Mixing Bowl.
2. Add egg whites, salt and pepper to the fish and mix thoroughly. Stir in the carrot and chives until evenly mixed.
3. Roll teaspoonfuls of the fish mixture into small balls, coating with cornflour to prevent sticking. Place inside the colander of the Multi-Server. Pour 1.7 litres (3 pints) of boiling water down the sides of the Multi-Server, cover and leave for 10 minutes. When cooked, drain and keep warm in the Multi-Server.
4. Gently fry the onion in the oil for 5 minutes. Add the tomatoes, tomato purée, vinegar, sugar and basil (if used), and cook for 10 minutes. Blend in a liquidiser or food processor for 30 seconds until smooth, and serve separately with the fish balls.

Makes about 42 balls

PORK AND CARROT BUTTONS

Preparation time : 2 hours 30 minutes
Cooking time : 10 minutes
Calories per button : 57

•

450g (1lb) boneless pork shoulder
175g (6oz) carrots, grated
1 small onion, grated
50g (2oz) fresh breadcrumbs

Crushed savoury biscuits, cornflakes and most plain unsweetened breakfast cereals make good substitutes for breadcrumbs.

1tbsp chopped fresh parsley (or 1tsp dried)
1tsp salt
1tbsp cornflour
1 egg, shaken in the Quick Shake
150g (5oz) ready-salted crisps, crushed into fine crumbs

Preheat oven to 200°C (400°F/Gas Mark 6)

1. Finely mince the pork or blend to a purée in a food processor. Transfer to a Multi Mixing Bowl.
2. Add the carrots, onion, breadcrumbs, parsley and salt, and mix well. Form the meat mixture into 3 sausages about 4cm (1½ in) in diameter. Dust with cornflour to prevent sticking. Place in a Freeze n Stor container and freeze for 2 hours to firm up.
3. Cut the sausages into 1cm (½ in) discs. Dip in egg and coat in crushed crisps. Place on a baking tray and bake in the centre of the oven for 10 minutes. Serve hot or cold.

Makes 40–45

BEEFBURGER NESTS

Preparation time : 30 minutes
Cooking time : 20 minutes
Calories per serving : 282

•

900g (2lb) lean minced beef
1 small onion, grated
1tsp salt
ground white pepper
25g (1oz) butter
450g (1lb) warm mashed potatoes
1 egg, shaken in the Quick Shake
75g (3oz) peas
75g (3oz) sweetcorn

Preheat oven to 200°C (400°F/Gas Mark 6)

1. Place the minced beef in a Multi Mixing Bowl with the onion, salt and a little pepper. Mix well and divide into 10 equal portions. Using the Hamburger Press, shape the beef into burgers and place on to baking trays.
2. Add the butter to the mashed potatoes and mix well, then add the egg. Mix thoroughly, and spoon into a piping bag fitted with a large star nozzle. Pipe a border on each burger, about 1cm (½ in) away

Always make sure you use good quality minced beef for burgers because they are cooked quickly. Tough mince means tough burgers.

TOP *Beefburger Nests* CENTRE *Tomato Fish Balls* BOTTOM *Pork & Carrot Buttons*

TOP *Fruit Yogurt Shakes* CENTRE *Ice Creamy Lollies* BOTTOM *Spicy Animals*

from the edge. Bake in the centre of the oven for 20 minutes until the potato is golden.

3. Boil the peas and sweetcorn together for 3 minutes, drain and use to fill the nests. Serve immediately.

Makes 10

The nests can also be filled with baked beans, spaghetti hoops or any other favourite fillings.

ICE CREAMY LOLLIES

Preparation time : 15 minutes
Freezing time : 5 hours
Calories per lolly : 66/92/123
•

Raspberry or Banana:
75g (3oz) fresh raspberries or
75g (3oz) ripe banana flesh
25g (1oz) caster sugar
175ml (6fl oz) evaporated milk

Chocolate Mint:
75g (3oz) plain chocolate
2tbsp chopped fresh mint
150ml (1/4 pint) evaporated milk

Double Chocolate:
75g (3oz) white chocolate
175ml (6fl oz) evaporated milk
15g (1/2oz) plain chocolate, grated

1. To make either of the fruit flavours, mash the fruit with the sugar, and make up to 175ml (6fl oz) with cold water. Add the milk and mix thoroughly.

2. To make the Chocolate Mint flavour, melt the plain chocolate and the mint with 3tbsp hot water in the Multi-Server (page 70). Stir in the milk and make up to 350ml (12fl oz) with cold water. Mix thoroughly.

3. To make the Double Chocolate flavour, follow the same instructions as (2), stirring in the grated chocolate with the milk.

4. Pour your choice of mixture into 6 Ice Tups, seal and freeze for 5 hours.

Each flavour makes 6 Ice Tups

Fruit cordials can also be used to flavour milk lollies. Mix 75ml (3fl oz) cordial, 100ml (4fl oz) evaporated milk and 150ml (1/4 pint) cold water.

FRUIT YOGURT SHAKES

Preparation time : 5 minutes
Calories per serving : 83
•

300ml (1/2 pint) fresh fruit juice (or puréed fruit)
150ml (1/4 pint) natural yogurt
50ml (2fl oz) milk
2tbsp vanilla soft-scoop ice cream

1. Place all the ingredients in a Quick Shake and shake vigorously to blend well.

2. Pour into glasses and serve immediately. The drinks may be decorated with slices of fresh fruit pressed over the edges of the glass.

Serves 3-4

SPICY ANIMALS

Preparation time : 1 hour
Cooking time : 40 minutes
Calories per animal : 60
•

225g (8oz) plain flour
1/2 tsp baking powder
1/2 tsp ground ginger
1/4 tsp ground cinnamon
1/4 tsp ground nutmeg
100g (4oz) unsalted butter
150g (5oz) soft brown sugar
1 egg
1tbsp milk

Preheat oven to 180°C (350°F/Gas Mark 4)

1. Using the Sift n Stor, sieve together the flour, baking powder, ginger, cinnamon and nutmeg into a Multi Mixing Bowl. Rub in the butter and add the sugar. Blend the egg and milk together in the Quick Shake and add to the flour mixture. Press to bind together, seal and chill for 30 minutes.

2. Gently knead the biscuit paste on a well floured Pastry Sheet until smooth. Roll out to 5mm (1/4 in) thick.

3. Cut out shapes with the hollow halves of the Animals from the Noah's Ark. Press trimmings together and roll out again. Bake on a lightly greased tray in the centre of the oven for 20 minutes. Allow biscuits to cool

Make a jelly mix and half fill the Colourfun Cereal Bowls. Seal and, using the tab, hang from bars in the fridge. When set you get half a bowl of jelly with room for fruit and ice cream.

Ice Tups
Make your own ice lollies for parties and special occasions, from fresh fruit juices or yogurt or other healthy ingredients. Stores neatly in the freezer until you need them.

for 10 minutes before transferring to a wire rack.

Makes about 36 animals

When cooled, the biscuits will remain crisp if stored in an Ultra Clear Jar VI.

NOAH'S ARK CAKE

Preparation time : 2 hours 10 minutes
plus overnight cooling
Cooking time : 1 hour 20 minutes
Calories per serving : 475

•

400g (14oz) self-raising flour
2tsp baking powder
400g (14oz) caster sugar
400g (14oz) soft margarine
7 eggs
juice and grated rind of 1 large lemon
175g (6oz) apricot jam (sieved weight)
650g (1lb 7oz) ready-to-roll icing
blue and orange food colour paste
icing sugar

Preheat oven to 170°C (325°F/Gas Mark 3)

1. Grease a 23cm (9in) square cake tin and line the base with baking parchment.
2. Sieve the flour and baking powder into a Fix n Mix. Add the sugar, margarine, eggs, lemon juice and rind. Mix thoroughly and then beat continuously for 1 minute.
3. Transfer mixture to the tin, smooth off and bake in the centre of the oven for 1 hour 20 minutes, until the top is brown and the middle springs back when gently pressed. (Do not open the oven door for the first 70 minutes of baking.) Leave to cool for 10 minutes, then turn out to cool completely on a wire rack.
4. Cut a strip 4cm (1½in) wide from either side of the cake. The centre section will form the boat. Trim the narrow ends to points to form the hull, undercutting slightly at the base to give a rounded shape.
5. Cut one strip of cake in half across. Butt together to form the house. Trim two long

triangles away from the top to form the roof. Sandwich the halves together with jam.
6. On the Pastry Sheet tint 250g (9oz) of the icing blue and tint another 200g (7oz) orange. Dust the Pastry Sheet and Rolling Pin with icing sugar and roll out the remaining white icing to about 15cm x 30cm (6in x 12in). Turn the icing over. Brush jam over the top of the boat, and place jam side down on the icing. Cut around the cake and lift it away with the icing stuck to it. Position the boat on the base of the Cheese Tray. Carefully brush the sides with jam.
7. Dust the Sheet with icing sugar again and roll out the blue icing to a rectangle about 14cm x 30cm (5½in x 12in). Cut two strips about 6cm x 29cm (2½in x 11½in). Gently score lines lengthways along the strips at 1cm (½in) intervals and use to cover the sides of the boat. Roll out the trimmings and cut two strips 2.5cm x 6cm (1in x 2½in). Moisten each strip with water and use to cover the joins at the ends of the boat.
8. Dust the Sheet and roll out the orange icing to a rectangle about 23cm x 20cm (9in x 8in). Turn the icing over. Brush one shaped end of the house with jam and place jam side down on the icing. Cut round the cake and lift off. Repeat with the other end. Brush the base of the house with jam and position on the boat. Measure the uncovered part of the house and cut the icing to fit. Fix in place with jam. Roll the trimmings out again and cut into 1cm (½in) strips. Use to cover the roof lengthways, overlapping each strip slightly from the bottom to the ridge. Roll a small cylinder for the chimney. Roll out white icing trimmings and cut windows and doors. Moisten with water to fix in position.
9. Place the Noah's Ark Animals and Ladder around the cake.

Serves 20

It is best to bake the cake a day in advance, as it is easier to cut and shape the following day.

Noah's Ark Toy
Colourful, fun and imaginative. The Noah's Ark captures some of the best qualities of Tupperware. The pairs of animals snap together for educational shape and colour matching. For safety, all pieces have gently rounded edges.

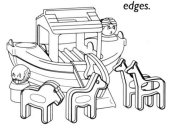

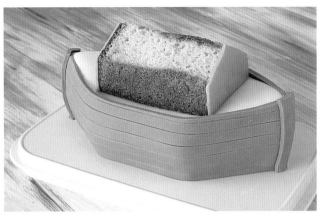

Noah's Ark Cake

Shortcrust pastry must be made using at least two parts flour to one part fat. The more fat it contains, the richer and more crumbly the pastry.

SHORTCRUST PASTRY

Preparation time : 5 minutes
Calories in total : 767

•

100g (4oz) plain flour
25g (1oz) butter
25g (1oz) vegetable fat
1-2tbsp ice cold water

1. Using the Sift n Stor, sieve the flour into the Multi Mixing Bowl. Cut the butter and fat into small pieces and, using fingertips, gently rub the fats into the flour.
2. Once there are no large lumps of fat, sprinkle 1tbsp water into the flour and, using the Paddle Scraper, start to bring the mixture together. Add a little more water and, using hands, press the mixture together to form a ball of dough, leaving the bowl clean.
3. Seal and refrigerate for 30 minutes before using. The dough can be made several days beforehand and stored in the fridge until required.

To bake blind (Cooking time: 20 minutes)

Preheat oven to 190°C (375°F/Gas Mark 5)

1. Lightly dust the Pastry Sheet with flour and roll out the pastry to the required size, turning frequently to form a round.
2. Using the Rolling Pin to support the weight of the dough, transfer the pastry sheet on to the flan tin.
3. Gently ease the pastry to fit the tin and trim off the excess.
4. Place a sheet of foil on to the pastry and weigh it down with dried beans. Bake in the centre of the oven for 10 minutes; then remove the beans and foil and bake for another 10 minutes.
5. Brush with a little egg white and cool before filling.

Make your own chocolates. Melt plain, milk or white cooking chocolate and add either coffee granules, peppermint essence, mixed nuts, coconut, crushed cornflakes or rice crispies. Harden in the Ice Cube Set.

PANCAKES

Preparation time : 3 minutes
Cooking time : 25 minutes
Calories per pancake : 54

•

150ml (¼ pint) milk
1 egg
50g (2oz) plain flour
1tbsp vegetable oil for frying

1. Put the milk and egg in the Quick Shake, then using the Sift n Stor sieve the flour straight on top. Seal and shake vigorously to blend.
2. Heat a frying pan until hot and brush a little oil on to it. Pour approximately 2tbsp batter into the pan, tipping the pan to coat the base evenly.
3. Cook over a medium heat until the edges start to brown, then turn over and cook the other side for 1 minute.

Makes approximately eight 20cm (8in) pancakes

CHOCOLATE CURLS

Preparation time : 15 minutes
Cooling time : 2 hours

•

175g (6oz) plain, milk or white chocolate
7g (¼oz) unsalted butter

1. Place the chocolate and butter into a Tropical Salad Bowl and melt in the Multi-Server by pouring 900ml (1½ pints) boiling water into the Multi-Server bowl and sitting the Salad Bowl in the colander. Cover and leave for 10 minutes.
2. Stir the chocolate and butter until smooth and transfer to a Half Square Round from the Mini Freezer Set. Seal and leave at room temperature for 2 hours to set.
3. Turn out of the container and, using a vegetable peeler, shave curls of chocolate from the block. Return the block of chocolate to the container and store in a cool place (but not in the fridge) for later use.

TOP *Baking blind* CENTRE *Shortcrust Pastry* BOTTOM *Chocolate Curls*

STOCKS

·

Vegetable:

1 medium onion, sliced
1 stick celery, cut into pieces
1 medium carrot, sliced
2 large sprigs parsley
1 bay leaf
6 peppercorns
600ml (1 pint) cold water

Fish:

450g (1lb) fish trimmings
900ml (1½ pints) cold water
1 medium onion, sliced
1 bay leaf
2 sprigs parsley

Chicken:

1 chicken carcass
1.2 litres (2 pints) cold water
1 medium carrot, sliced
1 medium onion, sliced
2 bay leaves
10 black peppercorns

Beef:

900g (2lb) beef marrowbones
1.2 litres (2 pints) cold water
1 medium onion, sliced
1 medium carrot, sliced
2 sticks celery, cut into pieces
2 bay leaves
1 large sprig thyme
10 black peppercorns

Method for making stock:

1. Place all the ingredients in a saucepan with a lid, and bring to the boil. Simmer for 10 minutes and then, using a Kitchen Duo Slotted Spoon, skim off any scum. Cover and continue to simmer gently for 15 minutes for the Vegetable Stock, 20 minutes for the Fish Stock, 45 minutes for the Chicken Stock, and 2 hours for the Beef Stock.

2. Leave to cool slightly and then strain before use.

WHITE SAUCE

Preparation time : 5 minutes

·

300ml (½ pint) milk
15g (½ oz) plain flour
½ tsp mustard powder
15g (½ oz) butter

1. Place the milk, flour and mustard powder in the Quick Shake and shake to blend.

2. Pour into a small saucepan, add the butter and bring to the boil, stirring continuously. Once the sauce has thickened, remove from the heat.

INDEX